planning
your wedding

planning
your wedding

hamlyn

confetti.co.uk

First published in Great Britain in 2007 by
Hamlyn, a division of Octopus Publishing Group Ltd
2–4 Heron Quays, London E14 4JP

ISBN-13: 978-0-600-61643-6
ISBN-10: 0-600-61643-6

A CIP catalogue record for this book is available from
the British Library

Printed and bound in China

10 9 8 7 6 5 4 3 2 1

contents

Introduction

Have you just decided to get married? Are you wondering where to begin and stressing already? Relax! This book will give you all the information you could possibly need and guide you through the whole wedding process from start to finish.

Because getting married is probably something you're not planning on doing too often, it's natural to want everything to be perfect. It's also natural to have moments when you panic. Don't worry – good planning is the key to making your big day run smoothly, and we're here to help you get organized.

Having the right attitude to your wedding is crucial. If you're worried that your grand passion will dwindle once you've committed yourselves till 'death do you part', that responsibility will drown the fun, or that things are just so perfect now any change has to be bad, think again. Yes, marriage will alter your relationship because, like everything else, relationships are always open to change. But change needn't be a bad thing – it can be a creative, positive force.

Whether you are the bride, bridesmaid, mother of the bride or anyone else involved in planning a wedding, we will tell you everything there is to know about putting together a legendary wedding day. The help starts well before the big day, taking you through everything from your engagement to the hen or stag night. We've got excellent advice on choosing a ring and announcing your engagement, as well as tips on how to throw a great engagement party. You'll also be thinking about how to celebrate your last moments of freedom – and we've got some exciting hen ideas to provide inspiration for chief bridesmaids.

The ceremony itself is, of course, at the heart of your wedding. Whether you're thinking about having a church ceremony, a civil wedding or a civil partnership, we can tell you what to expect. And if you want to do something different, you'll also find the low-down on getting married abroad and humanist ceremonies.

Each successful big day is made up of lots of carefully planned components. We'll take you through them all, from compiling guest lists to choosing flowers, photographers and stationery. Plus you'll find lots of advice on looking and feeling good throughout the day – from health and beauty tips to choosing the perfect dress and accessories.

We'll help you sort the all-important reception too, providing all the tips you need to make sure you get what's right for you and your budget.

The fun doesn't stop once the big day is over – there's the small matter of the honeymoon – and we've got lots of great ideas for that, too.

In fact, we've got everything covered to help you make your big day one to remember forever.

For more ideas and resources, including interactive to-do lists, budget planners and much more, visit our website (www.confetti.co.uk). There you will find expert advice to help you plan every aspect of your wedding, from choosing the right dress to buying insurance.

Having the wedding you really want

Make sure, right from the start, that you have the kind of wedding you want and don't be bulldozed into having a particular kind of wedding just to suit the wishes of your mum, dad, future in-laws, even friends. Before you start planning and discussing your wedding with others, think carefully about the following:

- State the ground rules clearly early on and make sure your family and friends know exactly what you have planned. Getting everything out in the open and stating your intentions as soon as possible will give you time to discuss thorny issues and clear up any disagreements at an early stage. This will minimize any disappointment, conflict or resentment later on.

- Be willing to compromise – a willingness to work together is what marriage is all about, and this is particularly true when it comes to planning your wedding.
- Agree a budget at the start. When your parents are paying for the wedding, guest lists can become an issue as costs can escalate. Let your parents know what you'd like, and then start to compromise.

- It is important to understand and respect the views of others, especially your parents. Arguing over whether to have a religious or civil ceremony, a traditional or off-the-wall one is to be expected. Your parents may have very different experiences and beliefs to you, and have been brought up with a completely different mind-set. But, equally, they should respect your beliefs and ideas.
- Remember, what you plan for your wedding day says a lot about who you really are. It's a time to be true to yourself, and sometimes friends and family will see a new side to you.

Keeping your cool

- Remember that an engagement is supposed to be an exciting time spent thinking about your betrothed and imagining the wonderful future you will have together.
- Decide with your fiancé early on who's going to do what and stick to what you agree.
- Try not to let the minute details become all consuming. Instead, delegate tasks to friends and relatives.

- Buy a wall planner and write down all the important dates or use an on-line wedding planner, such as Confetti's interactive wedding calendar (www.confetti.co.uk).
- Build some planning-free zones into your timetable, such as going out for a meal with your fiancé and agreeing not to mention the wedding.
- Don't worry about being too bossy or opinionated.

Most people you deal with, such as the caterer or the photographer, will appreciate it if you know exactly what you want and tell them so. Keep pictures of flowers/table settings/hairstyles and so on that you like in a file so that you have a visual reference to show people.

Setting the date

When deciding on a date for your wedding, you'll need to think about when you and your fiancé, the best man, bridesmaids and ushers, as well as important relatives and close friends, are free to attend. You might also want your wedding date to be one of special personal significance.

Most people get married on a Saturday (or a Sunday in some religions). This is a day when schools and most offices are closed, and so fewer people have to take time off work. Friday is the second most popular day, especially if you've set your heart on a certain month and your reception venue is already booked up for all the Saturdays.

The majority of couples get married in June, July or August because, allegedly, the weather is better then. Other popular times of year are Christmas, spring (especially April), early September and St Valentine's Day. Alternatively, what about a date that means something to you? The anniversary of when you first met or kissed. Your birthday. The birthday of your favourite film star. Pick a date, any date!

Once the wedding date is set, you and your fiancé should contact the vicar of the church in which you wish to be married or, if the wedding is to take place in a register office or civil venue, visit the Superintendent Registrar for your area. (See also pages 48–49 and 51.)

Keeping it legal

To be legally married in the UK, the following requirements must be fulfilled:

- You and your partner must be at least 16 years old. (In England and Wales, if either party is under 18 written consent to the marriage must be obtained from the parents or legal guardian.)
- You must not be closely related.
- The marriage must take place in premises where marriage can be legally solemnized. These include register offices, premises that have been given a civil licence by the local authority, parish churches of the Church of England and other churches that have been registered by the Register General for worship and marriage. There are exceptions for military marriages and for those who are detained or housebound.
- The ceremony must take place in the presence of a Superintendent Registrar, a Registrar or an authorized person.
- In England and Wales, the ceremony must take place between 8am and 6pm (except for the Jewish and the Society of Friends). In Scotland, you can marry at any time.
- Two witnesses must be present to witness the ceremony.
- You must both be free and eligible to marry.

Your
engagement

Choosing the ring

Most engagements are secured with the help of a big sparkler. Traditionally, the man pays for the engagement ring, and one popular guideline (admittedly perpetrated by the diamond industry) is that it should cost him two months' salary. It should be left to the individual to decide whether that's net or gross!

It's best to steer clear of second-hand rings, unless they are quality antiques or family heirlooms, and even then be careful. If you suspect that your partner is thinking about giving you a family heirloom, make sure that he knows your taste in jewellery and your ring size. If you call off the engagement, the ring should be returned. If your fiancé calls it off, you get to keep it, and it's up to you what you do with it.

Your fiancé should always keep the receipt, just in case you hate the ring he's chosen, turn him down or if you ever need to make an insurance claim.

Make sure your ring is insured as soon as possible. If your fiancé plans to pop the question abroad, he needs to make sure the ring's covered by travel insurance, in case it drops from his pocket en route to that tropical desert island.

Consider your wedding ring

Consider the type of wedding ring you want to wear, so you can be sure that your engagement ring and wedding ring will go together. Wedding rings are usually gold, white gold, red gold or platinum. The engagement ring generally looks more stylish if it is made from the same metal as the wedding ring.

Know your ring size

Have your ring size measured properly (in any jewellers). The ring should not fit too tightly as in hot weather hands swell and you won't be able to get it on or off. Equally, the ring should not be so loose that it slides around on your finger or over your knuckle too easily.

Don't rush your decision

There are thousands of styles of engagement ring to choose from, and it's worth taking your time to find the right one – after all, you will be wearing it for a lifetime and you'll want to love it just as much in the years to come. Shop around and make sure you buy from a reputable company.

Diamond guide

To help you choose the right rock, you'll need to consider the four 'Cs': colour, clarity, carat and cut.

The closer a diamond is to having no **colour**, the more valuable it is. The **clarity** of a diamond also influences its value. The fewer flaws it has, the greater its value.

The **carat** is a measure of weight, which also indicates the size of the diamond. Larger diamonds are rarer and therefore they are more valuable.

The **cut** of a diamond refers to the proportions that the diamond is cut to, and its shape.

- Round diamonds reflect almost all the light that enters them and are therefore the most brilliant. The round brilliant cut is the most popular diamond shape.
- Emerald-cut diamonds are rectangular and usually set with side stones.
- Pear or teardrop-shaped diamonds are shaped as the name suggests, and are popular for engagement rings.
- Oval-shaped diamonds can look particularly good on small fingers.
- Princess cut diamonds are square-shaped with untrimmed corners.
- Marquise diamonds are oval-shaped with tapered ends.
- Radiant diamonds are square-shaped with trimmed corners.

Announcing your engagement

You'll be keen to tell as many relatives and friends as possible the good news of your engagement. Compile a list of those you want to contact and then decide how you wish to inform them, whether by a visit, letter, phone call, e-mail or at a party. If you wish to make a formal announcement, it's traditional for the bride's parents to announce the news in the press. The usual wording is given in the following examples, but this can be altered easily to suit your personal circumstances.

Wording for a local newspaper

Mr and Mrs Robert Smith of Spring Cottage, Dover, Kent are delighted to announce the engagement of their daughter Anne Jane to Mark, son of Mr and Mrs Brian Shaw of Kingsbridge, Devon.

Wording for a national newspaper

The engagement is announced between Mark, younger son of Mr and Mrs Brian Shaw of Kingsbridge, Devon, and Anne Jane, only daughter of Mr and Mrs Robert Smith of Dover, Kent.

Getting in first

If you're planning on marrying at a very popular time of year or in peak holiday season, it's a good idea to send out 'save the date' cards. These can be very simple and read: 'Julia and Matt are pleased to announce their engagement, and hope you will save the date of 24 July, 2008 for their wedding.'

Having an engagement party

There's no set place or time as to where or when an engagement party should be held, but, in general, it tends to work best as an evening event. If, however, you want to make it a more informal occasion, perhaps with lots of children, there's no reason why it couldn't be held on a weekend afternoon.

The party can simply be a get-together in the family home, in which case it's traditionally hosted by the bride's parents. Alternatively, it can be a more formal affair in a hall with caterers or a private function room in a restaurant or pub. An engagement party is not a dress rehearsal for the big day, so don't feel that you have to invite all your relatives and your parents' friends and business associates to the event.

Things to consider

- Think about whether you want an intimate gathering with your family or a big bash with all your friends.
- Don't plan it too far in advance, or it could end up too close to the actual wedding date.
- First, check that both sets of parents will be free on the day you want to hold your party. For some couples, this may be the first chance for their respective parents to meet.
- Send out invitations one to two months in advance. If your parents are hosting the party, then the invitations should come from them.
- Even if you're holding the party at home, it's a good idea to hire caterers. Allow at least two months to book up caterers or a restaurant.
- If you're throwing an informal gig at home, you'll probably get away with a couple of party CDs. For a bigger event, it's worth hiring a professional DJ or even a live band or singer.

Hen and stag parties

Planning the hen party isn't the bride's responsibility – just as planning the stag party isn't the groom's. Brides (and grooms) have enough to do in the lead-up to the wedding, so share our advice with the chief bridesmaid and best man, or whoever is planning your event.

Traditionally, the bride or groom is kept in the dark about the hen or stag do, but to make sure you get a surprise you'll enjoy, drop some hints. Whoever is doing the organizing will be grateful to know the sort of celebration you want. They'll also need to check with you who you want to invite. Will it just be your closest friends, or are work colleagues and family welcome?

Think about the group's ages and interests as you may need to have different activities organized throughout the day, for example, beauty treatments at a spa followed by a nice meal, after which parents can leave while the young go clubbing.

Perfect planning

The night before the wedding is a definite no-no for hen or stag parties. The best time is at least a week before the big day, with both the hen and stag parties happening on the same weekend (although this may not be feasible if a lot of your friends have children). This means you won't lose two weekends together in the crucial last few weeks.

You'll also need to think about the party location. Do most of your friends live in one area, or is there somewhere central that's easily accessible for everyone?

On the day

Whatever you're doing, make
sure you pace the events. You've
got a whole evening – or even a
whole weekend – so don't tire
everyone out too quickly. If alcohol is
involved, don't let everyone drink too
much too soon. A nice meal in a
restaurant before you hit the clubs will
help with this.

Take a camera or a video with you to the hen or
stag party to record the fun. And don't forget that it's the
chief bridesmaid's or best man's job to make sure people
don't play jokes on you or the groom that might not seem
funny in the morning, such as sending you off on a cross-
Channel ferry or dyeing his hair blue.

Paying up

The costs of the hen and stag party should be divided among
the group. The bride and groom shouldn't have to pay for
anything. If you're going on a spa weekend, hiring a cottage or
doing anything that involves a group booking, a note/e-mail
can be sent in advance to everyone taking part asking for a
cheque to cover costs.

The chief bridesmaid/best man should make it clear to
other members of the party that unless they pay up, their
places can't be reserved! If you're hitting the bars, it's a good
idea for everyone to be asked to contribute towards a kitty
at the start of the evening – though as the bride or groom,
you won't be expected to contribute, of course.

The perfect hen do

Great hen party ideas

A hen night doesn't have to mean dressing up in a tiara and 'L' plates and going on a pub crawl. There are lots of other great ideas you could try:

- Have all the girls over for a sleepover, complete with takeaways, manicures and a few good chick flicks.
- Enjoy a day (or better yet, a whole weekend) of being pampered in a spa.
- Have a top chef come and cook a gourmet meal at your place. You can relax in your own home, be thoroughly spoiled, have the chance to watch the master at work and even pick up a few tips.
- Take the Eurostar to Paris and enjoy a weekend of designer shopping, clubbing and fabulous food.

- Spend a day being beautifully made over and then document your transformation with a glamorous photo shoot.
- If you and your mates fancy yourselves as the next Girls Aloud, book yourselves into a studio for a few hours' recording time with the latest equipment. Or hire a karaoke machine for the night and invite all your friends round for a go.
- Hold a US-style bridal shower, when the bride's friends and female relatives shower her with gifts!
- Spoil yourselves with afternoon tea and fancy cakes at a posh hotel.
- Take to the skies and go hot-air ballooning.
- Hit the town with an early evening show, followed by a night of pubbing and clubbing.

Hen and stag checklist

Don't let the logistics spoil your celebrations. To ensure everything goes according to plan, the best man and chief bridesmaid will need to do the following:

- Draw up a list of people to invite, in consultation with the bride/groom.
- Select a town/venue that's easily accessible to everyone.
- Decide on what kind of stag/hen party would be best for the people involved, establish an itinerary and make enquiries and then some provisional bookings.
- Pre-book everything possible so you're not thwarted by not being able to get into a venue/restaurant. Confirm bookings in writing (especially accommodation) and reconfirm the day before, too.
- Let invitees know well in advance if there's anything extra they should bring along with them – such as props, funny stories about the bride/groom, old photos, a change of clothes – and be contactable to answer any queries.

- Create and send out invitations.
- Make sure that everyone knows exactly where you're meeting. Give a contact number – ideally a mobile phone number – for any last-minute changes/confirmations.
- Make sure everyone knows roughly how much the do will cost – and that they'll be helping to cover the bride's/groom's costs. Let everyone know how and when payment is to be made.
- Have a fall-back meeting-place for late arrivals/people who get lost.
- Find out how everyone will get back home. Do you need to arrange transport/book taxis/send younger (or older) members of the party home earlier?

Working out your budget

There's only one real rule when it comes to budgeting for your wedding: plan for the type of wedding you can realistically afford.

The average wedding costs somewhere in the region of £14,000. Around £1,200 of that is spent on the rings, £1,400 on the wedding outfits and essential pampering in the run-up to the big day, and £1,300 on the wedding itself. The reception costs around £3,500 and, finally, of course, there's the honeymoon and other expenses that vary from couple to couple.

Traditionally, it falls to the father of the bride to pick up the tab for the main event, with the groom paying for the church or register office fees and the honeymoon. But more and more couples now choose to pay for the bulk of their wedding themselves. It's important to work out from the start who is paying for what and whether there are any financial constraints.

If your parents are contributing to, or paying for, your wedding, it's also a good idea to clarify exactly how much say they will have when it comes to organizing the event – the venue, the food, the music, the cake and the order of the day. They may feel it's only fair that they should play a part in the planning, rather than just being the ones paying the bills!

Often the groom's parents are pleased to contribute financially to the occasion in some way. However, this is not a foregone

conclusion, and you should not expect the groom's parents to share the bill or be offended if they don't offer to do so.

If the groom's parents make an offer and you are happy for them to contribute, then make a list of who's paying for what as soon as possible, to avoid any misunderstandings. One common solution is for the groom's family to provide the wedding cake and pay for any food at the evening reception. Or you may want to do a straight 50:50 split. Tread carefully, though. Ask them first what they have in mind.

How to split the cost of the wedding
The list below outlines who traditionally pays for what. Use it as a starting point to discuss who will do (and pay for) what as soon as you and your fiancé have set a date for your wedding.

The bride's family pays for:
- engagement and wedding press announcements
- the bride's and bridesmaids' dresses (many brides now pay for their own dress)
- flowers for the church and reception (except the bouquets and buttonholes)
- photographer/videomaker
- wedding stationery
- the reception and all that entails – the big expense!

The groom pays for:
- the wedding rings
- all church/register office expenses
- the bride's bouquet, bridesmaids' flowers and buttonholes for the male members of the wedding party
- transport
- presents for the best man, ushers and bridesmaids
- the hotel on the first night
- the honeymoon

Budget advice

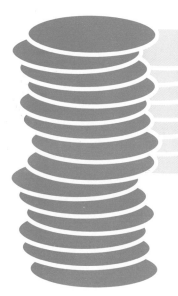

It is essential to set a limit to the amount you are willing to spend on your wedding, whether it's you or your parents paying. Add a further ten per cent to your budget to cope with any extras.

Manage your budget

Use the budget planner on page 156 to help you to manage the cost of your wedding. For an interactive budget planner, check out: www.confetti.co.uk

Open a wedding account

It is a good idea to open a wedding account and start paying in a regular sum each month, preferably by standing order or direct debit. All bills can be paid from this account and it is easy to keep track of how much is being spent.

Shop around

The easiest way to save money is not to pay over the odds. Ask for quotations in writing and make sure you know exactly what the price agreed covers. Remember that you may need to add VAT to some prices, so always ask.

Take out insurance

Wedding insurance is well worth considering. It will cover you for a number of eventualities, such as damage to your dress, cancellation of the reception (because of illness) and double booking of the venue. Bear in mind, though, that wedding insurance won't cover you if you get cold feet on the big day!

Wedding on a shoestring checklist

- Consider a weekday wedding, when venues may charge less.
- Check if you can supply your own wine for the reception. For your toast, opt for an inexpensive sparkling wine rather than champagne, then have a pay bar for the rest of the evening. If there's no bar at your venue, you could ask all your guests to bring a bottle!
- Hire your wedding dress, make your own or buy or hire a worn-once dress.
- Ask your mum or her friends to do the church flowers – and save on florist's costs. Seasonal flowers will be cheaper.
- Use a good photographer, but preferably one whose company is small enough not to charge VAT. Or ask your arty friends to take your photos. At the reception, put disposable cameras on each table.

- Make use of friends with posh cars to transport the wedding party to the church or venue.
- Invite more casual friends to an evening drink rather than the full wedding with all its catering costs.
- Ask a relative or friend with culinary talents to make the cake as their wedding gift to you.
- Forego the professional DJ and play your own CDs or tapes or ask an aspiring DJ friend to do their thing.
- You may even decide to ask your guests to chip in for your celebration, although for many people this is a contentious issue.
- Leave for your honeymoon on a weekday. Consider an all-inclusive hotel package.
- Ask your guests to give you honeymoon vouchers as a present.

Hiring a wedding planner

Considering that it takes a bride an average of 250 hours to plan her wedding, it's not surprising that many couples are deciding to find someone to do at least some of the work.

Wedding planners can help you have a fantastic day – without any of the hassle. Of course, using a wedding planner won't be for you if you or the groom want to be completely hands-on in every area of your day, or if your mum will be seriously put out if she can't do the organizing. But if you don't mind delegating, a planner can provide a perfect solution for a time-poor bride.

The services that wedding planners offer range from simply being there on the wedding day so they can coordinate the day itself for couples who have planned the wedding, to organizing everything from start to finish. A reputable planner won't take over your day – instead, they will work with you to decide what you want them to do and what (if anything!) you want to do yourself.

The most important thing when choosing a planner is to find someone you get on with. This is someone who is going to plan the most important day of your life, so it's essential that you can communicate well with them and trust their judgement. It's also crucial that the planner is on your wavelength and will be able to interpret your ideas properly.

Finding a wedding planner

Ask friends or family if they can recommend a good wedding planner. When shopping around for a planner, you should ask to see photographs/portfolios of their previous work. They should also be able to provide you with references and contact details of people you can speak to whose weddings they have planned. Once you're satisfied, you'll need to sign a contract.

Fees vary, but it's common for a wedding planner to charge between 10 and 15 per cent of the whole budget, depending on the size of the wedding and the amount of time they need to put in to plan it. It is possible that using a planner could actually save you a little bit of money because of their knowledge, expertise and negotiating power with suppliers. But the main thing a wedding planner will save you is time – giving you more time to spend together and more time to enjoy your big day.

What do wedding planners do?

The following services are offered by wedding planners:

- Designing the overall theme of the wedding.
- Finding the venue for the wedding/reception.
- Sourcing all the supplies, including flowers, invitations, photography, music and food and being the main point of contact for the suppliers.
- Going shopping with the couple to help choose their outfits.
- Being there on the big day to make sure everything goes according to plan.

Church
weddings

Church of England weddings

For most people, a church wedding means marrying in the picturesque church in the village where your parents live and where you probably grew up. However, marrying in a church is all about getting married in the eyes of God. If you don't believe in God, it would be respectful to think carefully about why you want a church wedding. Some vicars, but not all, don't seem to mind if you're not a regular member of their congregation and will be happy to marry you in their church.

What is a Church of England wedding?

The service is both a civil ceremony and a religious one, where you ask for your marriage to be sanctified in the presence of God. The vicar is legally registered to perform the civil ceremony as well as the religious rites. The service contains religious music and readings, although secular ones can be included if thought appropriate by the vicar.

Pre-wedding arrangements

Make an appointment to visit the vicar of the church and parish in which you wish to marry and sort out your marriage licence.

If the church is in your parents' or your own parish, your vicar will organize a licence for you. Otherwise, you can apply for a common licence, which requires you to be resident in your preferred parish for 15 days. You must also be able to give the vicar a good reason why he or she should agree to let you get married there. Unfortunately, aesthetic reasons don't count and, ultimately, it all depends on the vicar's

Different types of service

There are three different types of marriage service:

- The 1662 version is written in the old-fashioned English of that time, and the bride has to promise to obey her husband.
- The 1928 version uses more modern English, and the bride does not promise to obey.
- The 1980 Alternative Service Book provides a modern format and the bride can choose whether to promise to obey or not.

personal opinion. There is also a procedure for obtaining a special licence for exceptional circumstances. The vicar will tell you what you need to do. You will be asked to fill in a form with details of your births and occupations and those of your fathers.

At your first meeting with the local vicar, you should seek his/her consent if you would like another vicar, such as a relative or friend, to officiate at the service. Normally, the two vicars will share the service, the relative/friend performing the actual marriage, the address and perhaps the blessing.

As soon as the date of the wedding is fixed, the vicar may ask you to attend a few short meetings to discuss the religious implications and significance of the wedding service and marriage.

Publishing the banns

This involves the notice of your impending marriage being read out in church on three consecutive Sundays before the wedding.

If you and the groom are from different parishes, the banns will be read in both. It is customary for the engaged couple to attend at least one of the services when the banns are read to the congregation.

The wedding can take place any time within the next three calendar months after the banns have been read. If this doesn't happen, they will have to be read again.

What to expect from a Church of England wedding

A Church of England wedding follows a traditional format and depending on the type of church, the service may range from modest to quite elaborate and formal. During the ceremony there will be a service, hymns, religious readings and prayers. There is some scope to personalize the ceremony with the choice of readings (religious or secular) and hymns, but this must be done in consultation with the vicar.

Because Church of England weddings take place in a church, dress is usually formal.

Order of service sheets

Once you've agreed the service with the vicar, you can print the order of service sheets. The Christian names or initials of the bride and groom, the name of the church and the date of the wedding, are printed on the front of the sheet. Inside are printed the order of service and the words of the hymns. Make sure you order enough for all the guests, plus some spares.

Wedding rehearsal

A rehearsal for the wedding ceremony usually takes place a few days before the wedding or on the evening before, depending when the main participants are available. A rehearsal is essential, especially for elaborate weddings, so that the main participants know the procedure. You need wear only casual clothes for this.

Giving the bride away

Usually the bride's father gives the bride away. If the father is dead or not available, the bride can choose anyone she likes to accompany her down the aisle, or she may walk alone.

If you're faced with a dilemma over whether to choose your biological father or a stepfather who brought you up, you could always have both dads escorting you down the aisle, one on each side. Alternatively, if you feel that your mother has been the constant support in your life, why not let her give you away? Whatever you decide, make sure you take responsibility for your decision and let everyone know in good time what the plan is.

Inviting guests

If you're getting married in a small church, some friends may have to be invited to the reception only. If it's a large church, make sure you have enough guests to fill it.

Where guests sit

It is traditional for the bride's family and friends to be seated on the left-hand side of the altar and the groom's on the right-hand side. If you have a very uneven ratio of guests, ask the ushers to fill up the seats equally on each side as guests arrive.

Dress code

Most people opt for formal wear – a wedding is a great excuse to get dressed up. For the wedding party at least, the choice is generally morning suits for the men, and the bride and bridesmaids in whatever gorgeous creations the bride chooses. There is no strict dress code, but the general rule is to dress for the occasion.

What happens on the day

The wedding party should arrive promptly, with the bride and her father the last to arrive. As the guests reach the church, they are handed service sheets by the ushers.

The bride enters the church on the right arm of her father, or whoever is to escort her. Traditionally, she has her face covered with a veil. The bridal procession consists of the chief bridesmaid, bridesmaids and page-boys. The organist starts the processional music as the bride enters the church, and the groom, best man and the congregation rise. The priest stands at the altar rail or on the chancel steps. When the bride reaches the chancel steps, the groom stands on her right with the best man to his right and slightly behind him.

Usually a hymn is sung once everyone is in their place, then the priest states the reason for the gathering and asks if anyone knows of any reason why the marriage should not take place.

Having received the couple's agreement to be married, the vicar asks who is giving the bride away. The bride hands her bouquet to the chief bridesmaid, and her father or escort places her right hand in that of the vicar, who gives it to the groom. The bride's father then steps back into his place in the first row of the pews on the bride's side.

The marriage vows are taken first by the groom and then the bride, led by the vicar. The best man places the ring(s) on a Bible held by the vicar. He blesses the ring(s) and the groom places the ring on the bride's ring finger. The bride may also place a ring on the groom's finger. The vicar then pronounces the couple man and wife, although the full legal requirements are not met until the register has been signed. It is at this point that the bride may lift her veil, helped by the chief bridesmaid, and kiss her husband.

The bride and groom, followed by the best man, chief bridesmaid, their parents, bridesmaids, page-boys and any other witnesses then proceed behind the vicar to the vestry to sign the register. Even if photography is not allowed in the church, it is usually permitted during the signing of the register. The priest then hands the marriage certificate to the groom.

At a given signal, the organist will strike up a triumphant piece of music. The bride, on the left arm of her new husband, proceeds slowly down the aisle to the church door. The attendants follow in orderly pairs, followed by the best man and chief bridesmaid, then the bride's mother, escorted by the groom's father, and the groom's mother, escorted by the bride's father.

Making your vows

Getting married in a church offers you less freedom to write your own vows than if you're tying the knot in a civil ceremony. For Church of England weddings, you are required, by law, to perform a large part of the standard ceremony vows. Usually, the only part you're allowed to change is the 'obey' aspect and to opt for 'respect' rather than 'honour'. This will be at the discretion of your minister, who may help you rewrite certain parts of the vows.

To personalize the meaning of the ceremony further, most couples marrying in a church like to choose special hymns or readings, or write their own prayers.

Ceremony checklist

Points to consider

- Note that the vicar will normally discourage weddings during Lent (the 40 days before Easter).
- Marriages can take place on any day of the week, but they must be between 8am and 6pm, and the most popular day for a wedding, Saturday, may be booked up well in advance.
- Think about how many people the church will safely accommodate so you can work out your guest list with that in mind.
- Are photographs, tape recordings or videos of the ceremony allowed?
- What are the vicar's views on the use of confetti?
- What facilities are available at the church, including flowers and church bells?
- Is there an organist and resident choir, and what type of music will be allowed? Check with both the usual organist and vicar if you wish to bring in an outside organist, choir, singer or group, and discuss it with them.
- During the signing of the register, there is an opportunity to add your own individual touch with perhaps a small group or an individual singer performing some of your favourite music. Check with the vicar that he or she is happy with your choice!
- Discuss the order of service, hymns and readings (religious or non-religious) that you would like with the vicar, as he or she has veto.

Roman Catholic weddings

If you or your intended are Roman Catholic, even non-practising, you will usually be allowed to marry in a Catholic church on condition that you sign up to the following basic principles:

- You choose to marry freely, without external pressure.
- You intend to remain together for the rest of your lives.
- You intend to remain faithful to each other.
- You intend to have at least one child (unless the bride is past childbearing age).

Normally the wedding will take place in the parish of the bride and/or groom. You will need the written consent of your own parish priest in order to marry in another church.

If neither of you has any real religious convictions, it may be advisable to choose a different kind of ceremony.

What is a Catholic wedding?

The service is a religious one, which usually also covers the civil aspect of a wedding. If this is not the case, you will need either to have a Registrar present at the church or to get married in a register office beforehand. You may be married with or without a Mass (the full Catholic religious service).

Your wedding will be performed by a priest or, sometimes, by a deacon. If you have a friend who is a priest and whom you'd particularly like to perform the ceremony, it is usually possible to arrange this, even in a church where he does not usually operate. A marriage with Mass will usually last about an hour, without Mass about half an hour. You will be able to choose whether to have hymns or other music.

Pre-wedding arrangements

You should try and give the church at least six months' notice of your wish to marry. You will be expected to obtain the marriage licence yourself. The publishing of the banns is a formality that the priest will take care of.

You will need to see the priest of the parish where the wedding is to take place. He will want to talk to you about the Catholic teaching on the nature and duties of marriage, and you will usually be asked to attend four or five meetings. You will be asked to fill in forms about yourself and your family, your baptism, confirmation and First Communion, and provide a baptism certificate (available from the church you were baptized in).

If one member of the couple is not a Catholic, you will need to obtain a dispensation for a 'mixed marriage'. Usually this is granted readily by the parish priest himself. If one of the partners is not baptized, a dispensation for 'disparity of cult' will be necessary. This must be granted by the bishop and you will need to allow enough time for this to go through well before the date of the wedding. The priest himself will take care of the paperwork for you.

If the bride and groom are both practising Catholics, they may choose a Nuptial Mass, where they will both receive Holy Communion. Mixed marriages are usually performed outside of Mass, in a ceremony that includes readings and prayers but no Communion. The vows are the same, whichever version you choose, and the bride does not promise to obey.

What to expect from a Roman Catholic wedding

A Catholic wedding is a formal religious (and usually a civil) ceremony that follows an established, traditional format.

There will be readings, a sermon (usually relating to marriage), prayers and hymns. There is some scope to personalize the ceremony with the choice of readings and hymns (in consultation with the priest).

If both bride and groom are Catholic, there will be communion, but only Catholics should take part in this. Dress is usually formal.

Acceptable dates

Weddings during the season of Lent (the weeks before Easter) are not encouraged, although nowadays they will not be refused, except for the three days before Easter Sunday. (Strictly speaking, if you get married during Lent, you may not be allowed flowers or organ music, although many priests will not insist on this.)

Choice of readings

The priest will provide you with a sample of texts and possibly hymns during the preparation. The attitude to non-biblical readings varies from parish to parish. As a general rule, it is best to keep non-religious texts for a moment like the signing of the register, when they will not be seen to be 'competing' with the Bible readings. Some priests will follow the rules to the letter, however, and not allow even this.

Choice of music

In principle, all music should all be sacred. If the parish has an organist available, you may request their services. Remember, they will expect to be paid (ask the priest how much seems reasonable). If you have friends who play other instruments, they may be allowed to play, on condition that the choice of music respects the sacred character of the occasion and place.

Inviting guests

It is a good idea to check the capacity of the church before sending out invitations: don't choose a small country parish for a grand society wedding! There are no restrictions on who may be present. There is no compulsory dress code, for the couple or the guests.

Order of service

Most parishes help non-churchgoers to follow what is happening by providing an order of service booklet. Alternatively, it may be a good idea to produce a service sheet yourselves, once you have chosen the texts and hymns. Consult the priest on what should be included. It is often helpful to give complete texts, for instance for the readings, and for prayers such as the Lord's Prayer, where everyone will be invited to join in. Other items in the service can simply be mentioned in the order in which they occur, to help your guests follow the service. Indications on when to stand, sit or kneel are always useful.

Wedding rehearsal

A rehearsal for the wedding ceremony usually takes place a few days before the wedding or on the evening before,

depending when the main participants are available. A rehearsal is essential, especially for elaborate weddings, so that the main participants know the procedure. You need wear only casual clothes for this.

Where guests should sit

If you are having a Mass, and especially if it is at a scheduled Mass time, you may be joined by other parishioners who are not your guests. They will usually be discreet and leave the front rows for your friends and family.

Capturing the day

A photographer and usually video cameras will be allowed, although sometimes the priest may wish to impose restrictions on when and where filming can take place. Whether you will be allowed to use confetti varies from church to church, too.

Fee arrangement

It's customary to give the priest a donation for his efforts, which will have included a fair amount of paperwork. How much is down to you and what you can afford. About £50–£70 is probably reasonable; more is generous. The groom or best man, or sometimes the bride's father, will usually give the donation to the priest in an envelope after the service. It's customary to invite the priest to the reception, too.

Your vows

The Catholic marriage ceremony more or less dictates what your vows are. However, do discuss what you would like to say with your priest – there might be room for manoeuvre.

Unitarian weddings

Unitarianism is a historic non-conformist faith that emphasizes individual choice and deciding for yourself in spiritual matters. It is the ultimate broad church, and may be right for you if you are looking for greater freedom and flexibility with your religious ceremony.

Today's movement emphasizes the shared quest for meaning, rather than any specific beliefs. Members may come from a variety of religious backgrounds, their beliefs ranging from liberal Christian to religious humanist to New Age.

About 900 wedding ceremonies take place in Unitarian churches in Britain each year.

The Unitarian ceremony

Flexibility is key. The exact form and content of your ceremony are agreed between you and the local officiant – not any supervisory body. Most Unitarian ministers and lay officials are happy to supervise 'personalized ceremonies', where the aim is to 'do justice to the beliefs of a couple, rather than seeking to use set religious language which may have little meaning for those taking part'.

Unitarians are happy to perform ceremonies for couples of different faiths – for example, Christian and Jewish – and for divorcées. In fact, divorcées actually form a higher percentage of those getting married in Unitarian churches and chapels than for any other denomination or faith.

In the ceremony, references to God may be omitted in favour of other material, such as poetry, which may reflect your beliefs. Couples can choose their own readings and write their own vows – provided that the marriage wording remains. For Unitarians, such ceremonies remain deeply 'religious' because they deal with people's personal beliefs and convictions (conventional or otherwise) about life issues.

Common questions about Unitarianism

What's the legal position?
Wedding ceremonies in Unitarian churches are legally recognized by the state, provided there is an authorized person present – often a Unitarian minister or member of the congregation – and the minimum legal contracting words are included.

Do I have to be a member?
You do not have to be a Unitarian or belong to a Unitarian congregation in order to be married in a Unitarian church, chapel or meeting house.

How much does it cost?
The fee for a Unitarian wedding varies and is usually set locally, but it is likely to be comparable to what you'd pay to have your wedding in a Church of England church.

Blessings

Blessings are wonderfully flexible and are a great way to inject a religious dimension into an otherwise fairly secular occasion, but they don't have to be religious. A blessing can be a self-contained ritual that you can tailor to fit your own requirements.

You can have as small or large an audience as you like, or there could be just the two of you. For couples planning a small civil ceremony, a blessing gives you the opportunity to involve more of your friends and family.

What does a blessing involve?

A blessing is a short ceremony that takes place after the official marriage ritual – normally a civil wedding, as a religious ceremony generally includes the blessing. Unlike the marriage itself, a blessing is not legally binding – it's a spiritual way of symbolizing your commitment to one another.

A blessing service usually involves a reading, hymn or song and a prayer. You could include traditional wedding music or something that has special meaning for the two of you – there's a lot of scope for making the ceremony your own.

If you want a formal religious blessing, you must get a priest to perform it and it will normally take place in a church.

A service of prayer and dedication after a civil ceremony largely follows the same pattern as a Church of England wedding, though with a few differences. Banns are not called, there is no entry in the church's marriage register, the husband and wife enter together and sit together in the church, and rings are not exchanged.

If the blessing is immediately after the wedding, the bride and groom will be wearing their wedding outfits. Alternatively, if the marriage takes place in a register office, the bride may wish to change into a 'traditional' dress for the blessing.

Why have a blessing?

In the case of interdenominational or inter-faith couples, it's often tricky to satisfy the demands of both religions. One good compromise is for the couple to be married in one religious tradition and have a blessing in the other.

Since Catholics are not allowed to remarry in church, divorcées often opt for a blessing. Divorced Catholics usually get married in a register office and then have a blessing later in the day or a few days afterwards in church.

When can you have a blessing?

There is no time limit on when you can have a blessing. It's customary for it to take place very soon after the wedding, usually on the day itself, but some couples prefer to have their marriage blessed several days after the wedding. If you're getting married in a church, a separate blessing ceremony is not usually performed, but that doesn't mean it's not allowed – talk to your minister. It's also possible to have a blessing as part of a register office wedding – speak to your Registrar.

Organizing a blessing

First speak to the person you want to give the blessing. They should be a recognized official of whatever church or tradition you follow. Explain exactly what you want and discuss how best to go about it. Remember: blessings don't have to be conventionally religious.

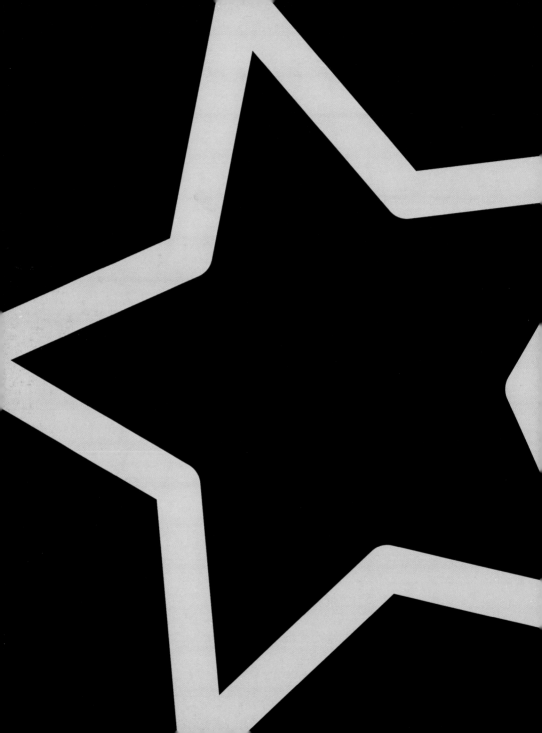

Civil
weddings

Civil weddings

There are many reasons why you might choose to have a civil wedding: you might have no religious beliefs, it could be your second marriage or perhaps you want to get married somewhere a bit different. Whatever your reason for wanting to tie the knot, no Superintendent Registrar can refuse to marry you, unless there is a legal reason to prevent it.

What is a civil ceremony?

- It contains no religious elements or anything with religious connotations (including no religious music).
- It is conducted and registered by a Superintendent Registrar or Registrar.
- It must take place after 8am and before 6pm, any day of the week, subject to staffing arrangements.
- The service can last anything from 10 to 30 minutes.
- The Registrar has to receive an 'Authority' for your marriage to be able to proceed, which can be obtained only by giving a Notice of Marriage (see page 51).

What are my options?

The classic alternatives to getting married in a church are in a register office or approved premises (licensed venues), but there are also other options such as marrying abroad or a humanist wedding.

Register offices These are local venues that are ordained specifically for performing weddings.

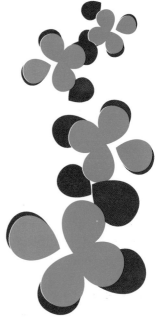

Approved premises These must be permanently moored, have a roof, be open for public use and be approved for use for weddings by the Superintendent Registrar of the district. The ceremony follows the same format as a register office wedding, except that you can make it more personal and slightly longer. Most approved premises are hotels and almost all of them will allow you to have the reception there afterwards.

Humanist wedding This ceremony isn't legally binding but it can take place absolutely anywhere. You can have a low-key register office ceremony first, then hold a humanist ceremony afterwards in your dream location.

DIY ceremony More like a party and not legally binding (couples must have a register office ceremony first), a DIY ceremony allows you to create the celebration of your dreams.

Marrying abroad 'Wedding packages' offered by tour operators can make this an inexpensive option, although many resorts have the reputation of offering 'conveyor belt' style weddings (see pages 58–65).

Civil partnerships These give gay and lesbian couples the same legal rights as a married couple. Like a civil wedding, a civil partnership registration is completely secular and can take place in a register office or another venue with a licence. The registration doesn't involve a ceremony, so if you want one you should discuss it with the registrar. You'll have the opportunity to say some words before you sign the registration schedule. As with a civil wedding, you'll need to bring at least two other people as witnesses.

Pre-wedding arrangements

You are entitled to marry in a civil ceremony at any register office in the UK or approved premise in England or Wales. You both have to give a Notice of Marriage in person in the district in which you live, even if you both live in the same district, and pay a fee.

Each party is also required to declare their nationality. This enables the Superintendent Registrar to advise you whether any further administrative procedures or legal requirements are needed to ensure the recognition of the marriage in the country of which you are a national.

A copy of the Notice will then go on display on a public noticeboard within the register office. Provided there is no legal objection, the Authority for your marriage will then be issued after 15 days, and is valid for a year from the date of your Notice. In other words, you can get married between 16 days and one calendar year from the day you give your Notice. It is your responsibility to ensure that both Notices will be valid for the date of your marriage. Visitors choosing to marry in England or Wales will need to satisfy the residential qualification of seven days and then wait a further 15 clear days before they are eligible to marry. Visitors to Northern Ireland must fulfil seven days' residency plus wait a further 21 days, while Scotland imposes no residential qualification but you must give 15 days' advance notice.

It all depends on whether you choose to marry in a register office or a licensed civil venue as to what happens next.

Notice of Marriage requirements
For the Notice of Marriage you may need to produce some or all of the following. All documents must be originals – photocopies are not acceptable.

- birth certificate
- passport
- decree absolute (if you are divorced)
- previous marriage certificate and spouse's death certificate (if you are widowed)
- any name change deed
- an item showing your current address, such as a driver's licence or utility bill
- parental, court or guardian permission (if you are aged 16 to 18)

For register office weddings

First of all, book the date with the Registrar. Although most couples choose to marry in their nearest register office, you may want to get married in a different one. Once you have your licence, make an appointment to see the Registrar of this other office.

If you decide to have readings or music in your ceremony, this is usually submitted and discussed with the Registrar prior to the service. You will need his or her approval.

For civil venue weddings

First, select the licensed venue you intend to marry in and check the availability of the Registrar at your local register office. Book them both. Find out from the venue what form the ceremony can take.

If you decide to have readings or music in your ceremony, this is usually submitted and discussed with the Registrar prior to the ceremony. You will need his or her approval.

What to expect from a civil wedding

A civil wedding can be as formal or informal as the bride and groom wish. For the ceremony itself, you select from a limited list of wording options. There is, however, scope to personalize your ceremony with readings and music that you choose, but everything has to be of a non-religious nature.

A civil wedding may include elements of 'church etiquette' such as bridesmaids, and the ceremony can be complemented by a religious blessing at a different time and place, if you choose.

Number of guests

Register offices and civil venues have a maximum number of guests that can be accommodated for safety reasons, and that includes babies and children. If the number of your guests exceeds this, you will need to decide who to ask to the ceremony and who to invite just to the reception.

Dress code

The bride can wear anything, from a smart outfit or full wedding dress complete with veil to fancy dress! And the groom could wear full morning suit or perhaps a lounge suit. Basically, the day is yours, so you have the option to be as formal or informal as you like.

Your vows

In civil ceremonies, you have more freedom to write your own vows – once the legal part of the ceremony is covered, then with the officiant's approval, you can add or subtract lines from the service. Many couples like to follow the standard vows, simply updating the words with language that's more contemporary.

Church etiquette

Many couples who opt to marry in a licensed venue adopt traditional church etiquette, for example by having bridesmaids and a best man. You can also set up an 'aisle' at your venue, meaning you can still be 'given away' in front of all your guests. The only real rule is that nothing with religious connotations can be incorporated into the ceremony.

What happens on the day

All those attending the ceremony should arrive in the building no later than about five minutes beforehand; Registrars are busy people and will probably have other marriages to conduct, so a prompt start is vital. In some register offices and most civil venues, it is possible for the bride to make an entrance on someone's arm without seeing the groom beforehand. Before the ceremony begins, the Registrar will see the bride and groom to check that the information stated on the Authority is correct and to ask for the names and occupations of their natural fathers. Any fees due will also need to be paid at this stage.

Humanist weddings

Humanists aim to draw positive moral values from life that are based on human experience, rather than God-given. They don't believe in an afterlife, but think that 'we should try to live full and happy lives... and make it easier for other people to do the same'. Humanist weddings are increasing in number each year. They are popular with people who have no religious affiliations but who want to enter into a publicly committed marital relationship.

What is a humanist wedding?

The British Humanist Association describes its ceremonies as 'dignified, caring, and totally personal' and publishes a practical wedding guide.

A humanist wedding is completely secular, with no hymns, prayers or Bible readings. This can be a particular advantage for couples coming from different faiths.

A humanist wedding can take place literally anywhere – from your front room to a mountain top. The rites performed have no legal status at all, so if you want to be legally married, then you'll need to have a civil wedding as well. However, some humanist ceremonies can now take place in certain specially licensed venues for civil marriages, incorporating a legally binding ceremony, performed by a Registrar, although there are limitations.

The BHA estimates that the total fee, including preparation, advice, rehearsals and the ceremony, is usually less than £150.

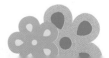

Organizing your humanist wedding

Once you have decided on a date for your wedding, you need to consider who you want to conduct the ceremony. A celebrant trained and licensed by the British Humanist Association (tel: 020 7079 3580 0908 or go to www.humanism.org.uk) usually conducts humanist weddings, but you can ask a friend or relative to do yours, if you prefer.

Next choose a venue, ideally somewhere that's significant and personal to you as a couple. You'll also need to decide whether you want to make the marriage legal by having a civil register office wedding first.

Decide on the type of service you'd like and what you would like to say. The job of the celebrant is to help you create a ceremony that's personal to you. They will help you to explore your feelings towards one another and to express them in words, devising your own vows. The ceremony can also include music, readings and any other symbolic actions you choose to make. You can write the entire service yourself to reflect the important aspects of your relationship or, with help and advice from the BHA, you can adapt one of the ceremonies they suggest to you.

Points to consider
- Find out how many people the venue will accommodate so you can work out the number of guests you can invite.
- If you decide to have the ceremony in a public place, make sure you find out if you can take photographs, arrange your own flowers, throw confetti and so on.
- Ideally, the venue should be available for a rehearsal a day or two before the wedding. Just wear everyday clothes to the wedding rehearsal.

What to expect from a humanist wedding

There's no set format for a humanist wedding – each ceremony is personal and unique. Remember though that humanist weddings don't have any legal status, so if you want to be legally married, you will also need to have a civil ceremony at a register office.

A humanist wedding can be held anywhere – inside or outside – and can be as formal or informal as you want. You can write your own vows and make your ceremony as creative as you like.

Inviting guests

The number of guests you have will be determined by who you want to invite and the capacity of the venue. If you are having a reception after the ceremony, you should make it clear whether your guests are invited to both or just the reception. It would be a good idea to include something on the invitation to describe what a humanist wedding entails.

Dress code

Because a humanist service is such a personal event, you can wear whatever you want. However, if you are having a civil wedding before, it is customary for the bride to wear smart day clothes, rather than the full white number, although there are no set conventions. You might be influenced by whether or not you have been married before, but you don't have to be. Brides can go for a white dress and veil with the men in full morning dress, although lounge suits are more usual for men.

Structure

Since there are no legal formalities to adhere to, the structure of the day is entirely up to you. This will, to some extent, have been rehearsed beforehand with the wedding party, so that the main participants know the procedure, their positions and when and where to move.

What happens on the day

This, again, has no set structure. At some point in the ceremony, you and the groom make promises to each other and, although they have no legal standing, the words will bind you together in love. A number of couples like to reflect on and celebrate their relationship before they make their promises. The majority of ceremonies will include readings and music, usually chosen for sentimental and personal reasons. The most important thing to remember is that the ceremony is about a public declaration of your love and commitment to each other.

Marrying abroad

The idea of getting away from all of the hassles of a home wedding and marrying abroad can be very attractive. Just imagine a sandy beach, blue skies, a warm breeze, palm trees and the sound of the sea gently lapping on the shore while you make your vows. If this conjures up a vision of romance in your mind, then getting married in an exotic location is for you. But there are plenty of other options to choose from, ranging from a 'drive-thru' wedding in Vegas to a ceremony aboard a Kenyan dhow floating on a Mombasa creek.

Keeping it private

Be aware that many hotels in exotic destinations perform more than one ceremony each day and you could also be the main attraction for hotel guests. Ask your tour operator or hotel for details, but if you want to be certain of a private ceremony, then consider a quiet or unusual destination.

Etiquette corner: Family considerations

By getting married abroad, you are bound to disappoint some members of your family and friends who cannot join you on the day, especially grandparents who might be too frail to undertake such a trip. To appease any objections, you could arrange to have a blessing service or reception when you return, but at the very least have a video made of the day, so that you can share your special moments with those unable to be with you.

Pros and Cons of Marrying Abroad

Pros

- It's much cheaper than the average British wedding. Many couples buy their own tickets and the bride's dad simply pays for the wedding package – it's acceptable for guests to pay their own way.
- You can invite just a small number of people with whom you really want to celebrate.
- If you book through a travel operator, they will do practically all of the organizing.
- If you opt for a tailor-made wedding, you can become very involved in the planning process.

Cons

- You may feel let down after the wedding and wish you had invited more family and friends along.
- Some people you want to invite may not be able to afford the ticket.
- You may upset those people you haven't invited.
- You won't have as much control over the organizing as you would at home.
- If it's just the two of you, a stranger will have to act as witness.
- Even if you head for tropical climes, you can't guarantee sunny weather.
- You might be stuck with your family on honeymoon!

Organizing a wedding abroad

Getting professional help

The most fuss-free way to organize a wedding abroad is to book with a reputable, bonded travel agent or tour operator specializing in arranging such events. These companies have dedicated wedding personnel who can answer all your queries and arrange every possible detail for you. Decide whether you want something exotic or more cultural, a hot or cold destination, how far you want to travel and a budget before choosing a destination.

Wedding packages are available in many hotels, with some offering a free ceremony if you stay a certain number of nights; others charge up to £1,000 or more. The service is nearly always civil, although religious ceremonies and blessings can be arranged in most destinations.

Packages tend to include just your basic requirements: the service, marriage licence, certificate and legal fees, but these differ from hotel to hotel. If you want extras, such as photographs, a video, flowers or a cake, then expect to pay more. Remember that any extras will generally be of a fairly basic nature compared to what you might expect if marrying at home. Always check in the brochure or with your tour operator for details.

Organizing a foreign wedding yourself

You can arrange your own wedding abroad but this will involve researching the legal requirements and residency rules and organizing all the finer details, from the ceremony to the flowers.

If you prefer to be in control then your first step will be to contact the consulate or embassy of the country where you intend to marry for advice. Always check with the tourist board of your chosen country that everything's fully legal and that you know exactly which documents you need to take with you to complete your dream civil ceremony.

Try to book a minimum of 12 weeks before departure to allow enough time for arrangements to be made and necessary documentation completed. More administration will have to be completed once you arrive at your destination, and this can take up to three days.

Residency requirements range from between zero and 40 days, so make sure you check these out before you go. Even with short residency periods, it is best to stay for at least a fortnight. This will allow you enough time to make the final arrangements and to relax after the ceremony and enjoy your honeymoon.

It is wise to take out additional holiday insurance that will cover every eventuality, from the loss of your dress to a hurricane preventing your wedding from taking place.

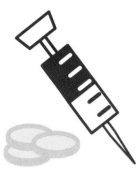

Health issues

Hygiene, health services and risk of disease vary throughout the world. You should take health advice as early as possible and ensure that vaccinations or preventative measures, such as malaria tablets, are taken in plenty of time to be fully effective by the date of travel. Get a copy of the free Department of Health leaflet E111 from your post office, GP or specialist travel clinic.

Validity of the ceremony

Do not rely on travel agents or any third party to ensure that the ceremony is valid in Britain. Check it for yourself with the local British embassy or consulate for up-to-date advice and information.

If you are not completely satisfied that your marriage will be recognized in this country, visit a register office in Britain to double check.

On your return home you do not need to register your marriage with the register office. You can use your foreign marriage certificate to change your name on your documents and with your bank, as you would if you had married in the UK. It is a good idea to obtain several copies of your marriage certificate, just in case you lose the original, as it is very difficult to get further copies at a later date.

Blessings abroad

If you are already married, be it recently or 25 years ago, many companies offer tropical blessings and renewal of vows services to celebrate your union. The only legal requirement is that you take along your original marriage certificate for authentication, although some destinations will require a photocopy of your certificate to be sent at least six weeks before you travel. Most of the services that are provided for weddings can be requested for your blessing service.

A different kind of wedding

- Enjoy a fairytale wedding at Disney World. Arrive in Cinderella's glass coach and have your photos taken with Mickey and Minnie Mouse!
- The Swiss lakes were made for romance – get married by tying the knot overlooking Lake Geneva.
- Opt for a drive-in wedding in Las Vegas – pull up at the hatch, and a minister will marry you through the window!
- Tie the knot in a hot-air balloon drifting over the South African plains.
- Head east for a traditional Buddhist ceremony in Thailand.
- Enjoy a snowy ceremony atop America's Heavenly Mountain, then ski down the slopes as husband and wife.
- Have the ceremony on the concourse of Sydney Opera House, overlooking the majestic harbour.
- Marry on an idyllic South Pacific island – you can't go far wrong with Bora Bora or Fiji.

Documentation

You and your fiancé will most certainly need to supply copies of the following before you travel, taking the originals with you to be produced before your ceremony:

- birth certificate
- ten-year passport, valid for at least six months after your return to the UK
- visa, if applicable
- affidavit/statutory declaration confirming single status, obtainable from a Commissioner of Oaths
- decree absolute (if you are divorced)
- previous marriage certificate and spouse's death certificate (if you are widowed)
- parental consent if you are under 18 (21 in some countries)

Marrying abroad checklist

- Think carefully about where you want to go, how long you'd like to be away, what kind of climate or special features you're looking for and how much you want to spend.
- Can your travel agent make any recommendations? Have they been to your preferred destination?
- What exactly is included in the wedding package?
- Will you be travelling in-season? What will the weather be like? Are there any discounts for travelling off-season?
- Where will the ceremony take place?
- Does the hotel restrict the number of weddings that take place each day?
- What happens if it rains? Can the date of your wedding be changed, or is there an indoor venue?
- Is the legal side properly covered?
- Can the airline guarantee you'll be sitting together?
- How much luggage are you allowed to take?
- Do you have the required travel visas?
- Are your passports up to date?
- Do you need to have any vaccinations? Should you start a course of malaria tablets?
- Do you have an adequate supply of regular medication?
- Have you allowed for extra travel costs: getting to the airport, extra port or departure tax, charges for travellers' cheques, passport renewal, extra cash for gratuities?
- How far in advance will you need to make the booking?
- What is the policy on cancellation/postponement?
- How much is the deposit to secure the booking and when is it due?

- When is the balance due?
- Is VAT included in the final price?
- Confirm dates, times and details with a written itinerary.
- If you're arranging the wedding yourself, does the hotel have an e-mail address, which will make communication easier and also avoid expensive telephone bills?
- Enquire at the country's consulate or tourist office about: residency requirements, necessary documentation such as proof of divorce or death of previous spouse, medical tests/vaccinations, witnesses and requirements for religious/civil ceremonies. Do documents have to be translated or notarized? How long will it take to process any paperwork?
- Does the venue have an in-house wedding coordinator?
- Can you arrange for safe transport of your wedding dress?

- Are discounts offered if you are booking blocks of hotel rooms for guests travelling with you?
- Are you able to meet your officiant before the ceremony?
- Will the ceremony be in English? Can you write your vows?
- Are you able to have your ceremony and reception at the same venue?
- Will the venue be decorated? How?
- How many guests can attend the ceremony? The reception?
- What reception packages are available? Are the menus flexible? Can they provide music/entertainment?
- Will the marriage certificate be given to you on the day of the ceremony or will it be sent to you later?
- Can you take out extra wedding insurance on top of your standard travel/honeymoon insurance?
- If you want to bring your own cake, check that it will be allowed into the country and that it will survive the flight.

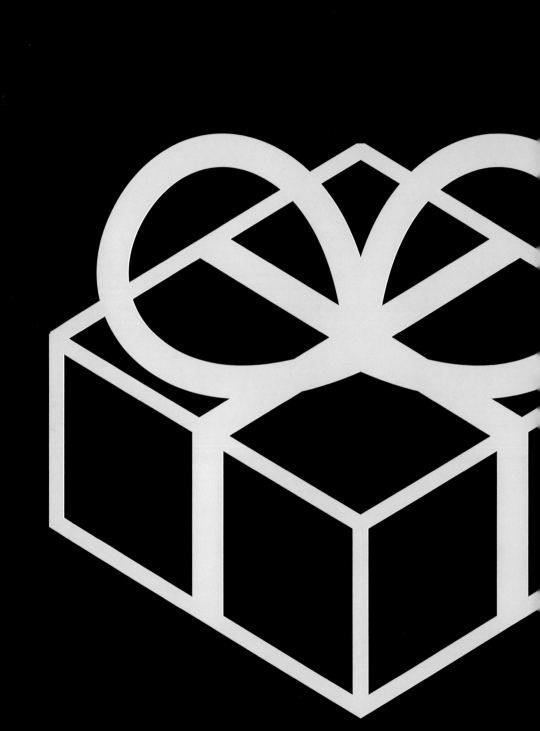

Guests, stationery
and gifts

The guest list

Deciding on the guest list is usually when the wedding party comes to blows! While invitations are traditionally sent out by the hosts (usually the bride's parents), the bride and groom should have the chance to each invite a similar number of guests. One way to do it is to split the list into three – one third for the bride's family, one third for the groom's family and one third for the couple's friends.

Start by asking everyone involved to make a rough list of guests, then start pruning. Ultimately, whoever is paying for the wedding should have the final say on numbers, but really the hosts and couple should have the final say on who gets on the list!

You should add the names of the minister and his or her partner to your list as a matter of courtesy, and when it comes to working out numbers, make sure you include all members of the wedding party – people sometimes forget to add themselves!

If you have relatives who you know won't be able to make it on the day, you obviously don't need to include them on your guest list, but make sure you send them an invitation. Many people, in particular elderly relatives, really appreciate this gesture – it shows that you haven't just forgotten or ignored them.

Keeping numbers down

If your wedding venue is too small to invite all the people you'd like to, ask them to celebrate with you after the marriage at the reception. No one should take offence at this arrangement. It's not a cheap solution, though, and the major factor for limiting numbers may well be cost rather than space.

If money is more of an issue than space, you can limit the number of guests you invite to the wedding breakfast to close family and friends, and then ask everyone else to join you in the evening celebrations, if that is an option.

Not inviting children will also help to reduce numbers, but make sure that you inform all the parents well in advance to give them time to get used to the idea and to organize childcare (see also page 73).

Stationery

Your wedding stationery can be just a simple card invitation or you can push the boat out and have a complete wedding pack – it all depends on you and the style of your wedding.

Designing the invitations

Your invitations can set the style for your wedding, whether traditional or out of the ordinary. You can find designs to suit all tastes and budgets from good stationers and local printers, or you can buy some card and create your own.

The classic wedding invitation is simply type (no graphics), ideally engraved on good-quality white or cream card. The format is an upright, folded card with the wording on one side. Black or silver lettering is the most popular.

You can buy ready-printed cards and fill in the details by hand, create your own design and have a set of invitations printed off or create each invitation individually. If you choose a traditional specially printed or engraved card, the guest's name is handwritten at the top left-hand side of the card.

How you break up the lines on the invitation is up to you. Generally speaking, however, names, times and places are placed on separate lines. Bear in mind that fairly equal line lengths usually look better on the page than an array of different ones.

Ordering and sending invitations

Ideally, you should order the invitations at least three months before the wedding and as soon as you have an idea of the number of people attending.

Allow one invitation per family, including a courtesy one for the groom's parents and the minister and his wife. Also include family and friends whom you may already know cannot come, but who would appreciate receiving an invitation anyway.

Don't forget to order a spare 20 or so invitations to allow for mistakes when writing them and for any extra guests you may decide to ask at a later date.

The invitations should be sent out at least six weeks before the wedding to give you as much time for organization as possible. Between 10 and 12 weeks before the wedding is average.

Reception invitations

If you are sending out invitations for the wedding reception or evening reception only, these can take the same form as any usual party invitation.

Traditional invitations

It is entirely up to you and your fiancé how to word your invitations. After all, it is your wedding day, and if you want the invitations to have only your names on them, so be it.

If you want to follow the traditional invitation style, there are several basic rules to follow:

- Invitations always go out from whoever is hosting the wedding, which is normally the bride's parents.
- Invitations are generally written in the third person, such as Mr & Mrs Jones, rather than 'we'.
- When you're listing the time, date and venue on your invitation, the time and date should be written first, the venue last.
- Use titles, for example Mrs, Dr, Sir, etc., when appropriate. There is no need for a full stop after Mr, Mrs or Dr.
- 'The honour of your presence' or 'the pleasure of your company' is the normal choice of wording. The former is often used for invitations to religious ceremonies, such as a church wedding, while the latter is preferred for invitations to an event in a non-religious location.
- The bride's name should appear before the groom's.

Other useful things to mention

It's also a good idea to include relevant information, for example:

- any dress requirements, such as black tie or smart dress
- whether food will be served (if it's not a dinner/lunch party)
- when the reception will finish
- whether drinks are free for the entire reception

Inviting children

On the invitations, make it quite clear to parents that their children are invited by including their names and let them know up front if you have made special arrangements for them, such as: 'We have arranged child-minding facilities for the duration of the service and/or reception.'

There are two ways of letting people know that children are not invited. The first is to tell parents tactfully before the invitations go out. The second way is to enclose a short note to parents, tactfully saying something like: 'We are sorry that we are unable to invite babies and children to the wedding.' Not only does this make the situation clear, but it also implies that your decision was due to circumstances beyond your control. Printing 'no children' on the invitations is not an option.

Alternative wording

If the bride's father is widowed:

Mr James Jones requests the pleasure...

If the bride's parents are divorced:

Mr James Jones and Mrs Pamela Jones request the pleasure...

If the bride's parents are divorced and her mother remarried:

Mr James Jones and Mrs Pamela Matthews request the pleasure...

If you're hosting your own wedding:

Ms Mary Alice Jones and Mr Carl David Spencer request the pleasure of your company at their marriage, etc.

Other stationery

Response cards

Many people word their invitations to include an address to which guests can reply, but the best way of ensuring a quick reply is to send a response card with the invitation, which can be completed and posted back to you.

As an alternative, you could buy a set of ready-printed RSVP cards – something plain and simple that won't clash with your invitation design – or buy plain card and write them yourself.

It's also a good idea to add a date by when you would like to receive the replies. A sensible date is one or two months before the event, or whatever suits your arrangements. After this date, start ringing round any stragglers for their answers.

Map and directions

The more detailed and carefully written the directions, the fewer phone calls you'll get from people who've got lost! The map can be drawn by hand, photocopied or printed from a map web site. You may also like to include details of the nearest train, tube or bus stations, as well as the numbers of local cab firms.

Local accommodation

For those travelling some distance, you can include a list of local hostels, B&Bs and hotels. Many hotels will allow block reservations of rooms, as long as they are confirmed by a certain date. This usually allows you to negotiate a more favourable rate, especially during the off-peak season.

Order of service

If you're having a church wedding, the sample template below should help you to set out your order of service. Make sure that you check the content with whoever is conducting your service before having these printed.

Wedding gift list

Traditionally, this isn't included with the invitation; guests who wish to buy the bride and groom a present ask the bride's parents for details about the gift list. However, nowadays it's more acceptable to include the gift list with the invitation.

If circumstances change

Hopefully you won't have to postpone or cancel your wedding, but if you do, you need to let your guests know formally. The usual wording for postponement and cancellation is given below.

For postponement

Owing to the recent illness of Mrs Jones, the wedding of her daughter Susan to Mr Neil Wood at St Mary's Church at 2pm on Saturday 5th April, 2003 has been postponed to 3pm on Saturday 12th August, 2003.

For cancellations

Owing to the sudden death of Mr Jones, the wedding of his daughter Susan to Mr Neil Wood will not now take place at St Mary's Church at 2pm on Saturday 5th April, 2003. The marriage will take place privately at a date to be decided.

Order of service

Front page
- *Church and location*
- *The marriage of bride and groom*
- *Date and time*

Inside page
- *Entrance music (processional) for bride*
- *Introduction*
- *Hymn (include words)*
- *The marriage*
- *Prayers (optional)*
- *Reading (optional)*
- *Blessing (optional)*
- *Hymn (include words)*
- *Reading/blessing (optional)*
- *Hymn (optional – include words)*
- *Signing of the register*
- *Exit music (recessional)*

Gift lists

Gift lists are one of the fun parts of planning a wedding. Most guests welcome advice on what to buy, so make your list as comprehensive as possible to cover a price range that will suit all pockets.

For first-timers

A young couple setting up home together for the first time will want all the basics: china, pots and pans, bed linen and glassware, even the humble lemon squeezer.

For late starters

Couples getting married a little later in life may already own a property or be living together, and are likely to have most of the staple household items. In this situation, couples often ask for more luxurious items they couldn't afford themselves.

Not for the first time

If you are getting married for the second or third time, you are even more likely to have amassed all the necessary household possessions. So, if you are both passionate about something, say entertaining friends, you could give your gift list a cooking theme and ask for specialist kitchen implements.

Money as a gift

Research shows that most guests are quite happy to give money as a gift, but they would prefer to know what it will be spent on – preferably something memorable or interesting. Couples have several options: they can receive money, vouchers or open an account for gifts. Alternatively, some websites, such as confetti.co.uk, allow couples to set up a wish list on line. A wish list lets guests contribute to the list and gives the couple the freedom to choose gifts from a variety of sources.

Gifts for the wedding party

Remember that you're not the only ones to receive gifts. It's traditional for the mothers, best man (sometimes the ushers), bridesmaids, flower girl, page-boy and any helpers to be given presents as well. The groom usually gives them during his speech at the reception. It's also up to him to give a general thanks to all the guests for your wedding gifts. You may also want to exchange gifts with your fiancé, which you can do either the day before the wedding or during the reception.

Points to consider

- Include a variety of gifts that will appeal to all tastes and pockets, so that no one feels pressured into buying something they don't like or can't afford.
- Don't just think of the here and now – think ahead. You may not be interested in a fancy cutlery set at the moment but in later years one could come in useful.
- If you want to have your wedding list at a large department store, make sure you find out when you can register, as some stores restrict registration to certain times.
- Although wedding etiquette demands that the gift list is not sent with the invitations, in practice many couples do so or at least refer to it – it's easier for everyone concerned.
- Keep a record of all the people who give you presents, so that you're prepared when it comes to writing your thank-you letters.

Looking beautiful

Looking beautiful

From ancient times, the bride has been celebrated, in poetry and prose, as everything good, pure and beautiful. That's some image to live up to! In reality, being a bride can be a very stressful experience. However natty your fiancé looks in his waistcoat and tails, you know that all eyes will be on you as you walk up the aisle.

Every bride wants to look and feel beautiful on her wedding day. But as well as having a flattering hairstyle and expertly applied make-up, beauty is all about being healthy and feeling relaxed. In this chapter, you'll find out how to pace your bridal beauty countdown, so that you look and feel your very best on the big day.

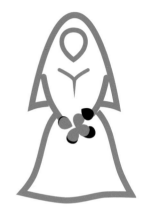

Take a good look at yourself

When you imagine your perfect wedding day, do you see a realistic image of yourself? We all want to look our most gorgeous for the big day – glowing, beautiful and with the body of a Hollywood starlet. But when the daydream fades, we know that most of us don't look much like the celebrity icons of glossy magazines. Worried? Don't be. Beauty comes in all different shapes and sizes, and the way to look your best is not to conjure up a picture of someone you're not – but to concentrate on the real image of yourself.

The dress

Your ultimate beauty accessory is your wedding dress. Buying one is great fun, but it can also be overwhelming simply because there's so much choice. Don't worry – we've got some great tips on how to find the perfect dress for you (see pages 88–91).

When choosing a dress, think about what you normally wear, your favourite colours, where the ceremony's taking place and the tone you're aiming for – traditional, avant-garde or relaxed. Once you have a clear idea of these elements, you can start applying them to your outfit.

Getting into shape

You want your body to be at its best on your wedding day, but the solution isn't to starve yourself. With a healthy diet, exercise and a little bit of professional help, you'll be a truly radiant bride.

You may have decided to lose a few pounds before your wedding day, but don't set yourself unrealistic targets. It's never easy to stick to a diet, and when you're feeling stressed, it's even harder.

Effective dieting isn't about calorie counting, it's about changing your eating habits. So tuck into more high-carbohydrate foods (cereals, bread, rice, pasta, potatoes) and fewer high-fat foods (cheese, ice cream, red meat, fried breakfasts). Get into the habit of eating like this all the time and aim to lose 500 g–1 kilo (1–2 pounds) a week.

Try to take some extra exercise, such as walking to work or swimming. This should burn off a few pounds but, more importantly, it will make you feel healthier and more relaxed.

If your budget allows, you might like to treat yourself to a few days at a health spa. Expert advice, beauty therapies and exercise facilities will help you come away feeling great.

Planning your look

For the big day, the idea is to look like a better version of yourself rather than going for a completely new look, so learn the trick of enhancing your best features.

Get into a regular skincare routine a few months before the wedding. Invest in some good products, and cleanse, tone and moisturize every morning and evening. To find out which products suit your skin, have a makeover in a department store. You'll receive lots of help and advice, and the fee is usually redeemable against any products bought.

The professionals

Nutritionist

If you're really serious about changing your eating habits and getting into shape for your wedding, you may want to consult a nutritionist.

A nutritionist will look at your lifestyle and diet, find out what your objectives are, and give you advice on what you should eat or avoid to help you look and feel your best on your big day.

Nutritionists tend to be holistic in their approach so you'll probably also be given advice on how to be more active and how to generally make your lifestyle more healthy. You'll need to see a nutritionist early in the run-up to the wedding, bearing in mind the amount of weight you want to lose and when your dress fittings are scheduled.

Check that your nutritionist is registered with a reputable professional organization and be wary of anyone who says they can help you lose more than two pounds per week.

Make-up artist

Using a make-up artist is a really good idea, especially if you don't usually wear make-up and need an experienced touch! Independent make-up artists will carry out a trial run a month or so before the big day, then come to your home on the morning of the wedding to recreate the look. Prices can vary substantially, so make sure you get a written quotation in advance that states exactly what is included. You could try to negotiate a discounted rate for your mum and bridesmaids to have their make-up applied professionally as well.

Hair stylist

Start thinking about your hairstyle as soon as you've set a wedding date. Don't be tempted to go for a dramatically different do for your wedding day, though – remember that even though the hairstyle won't last forever, your photos will!

Book a consultation at a couple of local salons until you find a stylist you feel comfortable with and who understands your hair type. Remember to take along as much information about your special day with you as possible – for example, a photo of your dress and a fabric sample to give the stylist a good idea of the look you're hoping to create.

Don't buy your tiara or veil until you've spoken to your hairdresser – his or her input can be invaluable.

Hair checklist

- Book your appointment in advance.
- Have at least one style rehearsal a month before the wedding. This will give you time to make alternative arrangements if you aren't comfortable with the style.
- Be honest with your stylist. You should feel comfortable expressing what you do and don't like.
- Leave plenty of time for your appointment – 2½ hours should do it. This is not a day to rush!
- Get your hair in tip-top shape. Plan regular weekly visits to the salon for trims and conditioning treatments two months before the wedding.
- If you've given nature a little hand with the hue of your locks, colour your hair three weeks before the ceremony to prevent roots showing.
- Keep in mind that your style has to last the entire day.
- Don't experiment on your wedding day.

Beauty countdown

Follow this beauty countdown to ensure that you will look your best on your big day.

- **12 weeks to go** Facial and shaping of eyebrows to complement the face; waxing; hair cut for wedding style; finish with a relaxing neck and back massage to unwind.
- **10 weeks to go** Manicure and pedicure – strengthening and conditioning nails as well as moisturizing skin on hands and feet.
- **7 weeks to go** Facial; waxing; neck and back massage.
- **5 weeks to go** Manicure and pedicure – experiment with nail colours.
- **3 weeks to go** Final hair cut and colour.
- **1 week to go** Facial (you should now be seeing the results of regular facials); waxing; neck and back massage.
- **2 days to go** Manicure and pedicure for final shaping of nails and conditioning of skin; trial wedding make-up to establish the look that suits you.
- **Wedding day** Set aside plenty of time for doing your hair and make-up; paint fingernails and toenails first and make sure they dry completely then do your hair and make-up.

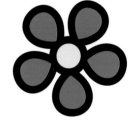

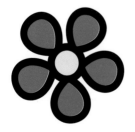

Choosing your dress

Although you've probably got lots of ideas and may well have been dreaming of the perfect dress for months, even years, it's best to seek out some professional advice. This will ensure that the final creation fits and flatters you perfectly, accentuating your good points and minimizing the rest.

A formal long dress is equally suitable for a church or civil ceremony, although many brides prefer to wear a smart dress or a suit for a register office wedding. If you're having a religious ceremony, bear in mind that some religions frown on sleeveless or very low-cut outfits.

Whatever style you decide on, it's worth remembering that the back view is as important as the front – for most ceremonies, the guests will be behind you. It's a good idea to choose fabric resistant to crushing and creasing. If you want to have a train, it's wise to make it detachable so that

it can be removed (or hooked up) for dancing at the reception.

Discuss your ideas with the groom to ensure that the colour and style are coordinated with him and all the attendants. There is no need to reveal the finer details of the dress, as traditionally these should not be known by the groom until he sees his bride walking up the aisle towards him.

Remember, a white dress isn't obligatory. If white doesn't suit your complexion or tastes, don't wear it. Wedding gowns in cream, pale gold, pale blue and pink are all quite usual now, and there's been a recent move to much deeper colours in shades of green or even burgundy – particularly stunning for a winter wedding.

If you decide against white, you shouldn't feel obliged to plump for a 'trendy' colour either. Far better to go for a dress in your favourite shade or one that makes your skin glow. Remember, though, that if you're going for a very bright colour, you should keep the detail on your dress to a minimum.

The right dress for your shape

Choosing a style that suits your body shape will make a huge difference to how you look, and it will also boost your confidence no end.

If your body or choice of ceremony isn't right for a white puffy dress, don't even think about trying one on. Not only will it depress you, but you might still buy it because of that traditional image you have in your head – and then you'll end up feeling awful on your big day.

- **If you are tall and slim** you could choose a ballgown with a strapless, fitted bodice.
- **If you are thin** and feel that your shoulders are rather bony or that your collarbone protrudes too much, go for a long fitted dress, perhaps with a high neckline. You may feel that you are too thin for this style, but your height and leanness could be set off with some delicate detailed embroidery or beading.

- **If you are short** with a fuller, feminine figure try an empire line dress. The beauty of this style is that it has a seam under the bustline and, in the right fabric, the dress will not cling to your body but flow around it. Although a knee-length dress could also look good, this longer shape will give you a taller silhouette. If you choose to have sleeves, go for long and narrow but not too tight.
- **If you have a very full bust** draw attention away from it by having a long bodice. Dresses that use the natural

waistline, on the other hand, will draw attention to the bust area. Make sure your bodice area is very plain, and avoid low necklines. If you are really keen on detail, save it for the hem of the skirt.

- **If you have full or wide hips** then avoid a bustle, peplum or anything tiered. Most styles of dress will look great, but make sure it's something that doesn't fit too tightly over the hip area. The 'princess' style, which is fitted on top and then flares slightly to the hem, will disguise larger hips. Even the ballgown look, in quite a simple material, will draw attention away from the hips.

- **If you have wide shoulders** consider narrowing your look with wide straps, or cover them completely and draw the focus to a V-neckline. It's important to show some skin around this area, but you can soften the effect by wearing a sheer wrap around your shoulders. Stay away from puffed sleeves!

- **If your legs are short** or on the heavy side it's a good idea to opt for a long dress. Give yourself more height with a sheath style, which is straight, but not too body-hugging.

- **If your arms are on the short side** then three-quarter-length sleeves will help to make them look longer, but, whatever you do, do not go sleeveless.

- **If your arms are chubby** go for long and simple sleeves that aren't skin tight.

Choosing between a shop-bought or homemade dress

As it is so important to find the right dress for you, it makes good sense to start dress-hunting up to 12 months before the ceremony, especially if you've set a date during the busy summer months. Brides have a few options to choose from, which include ready-made, made-to-measure and couture dresses. The final dress fitting should be about two weeks before the wedding.

The cost of dresses varies greatly, so have a clear idea of how much you are prepared to spend before you go shopping. It is best to try on as many different styles as you can at first and view them from all angles. Take along a trusted friend for honest advice, and don't feel pressured by salespeople. Take your time to choose and enjoy the shopping spree!

Specialist bridal shops and stores keep dozens of styles in a range of sizes and most provide a fitting and alteration service at a small extra cost. You may need to book an appointment in some of the most popular shops.

If you feel that buying a dress is too extravagant, hiring a dress or wearing a worn-once dress is a popular option, and specialist hire shops offer an extensive range to suit all pockets.

If you can't find the dress of your dreams at a bridal or hire shop, you may have to get it made or make it yourself.

First, consider whether you feel confident enough to make your own dress. It may be far better to choose a pattern and material and employ a professional dressmaker. Your dressmaker should be happy to incorporate your

individual preferences and finishing touches, such as lace inserts, ribbons and embroidery.

You ought to get several fittings, and some dressmakers will even visit you on your wedding day to make last-minute adjustments. All this costs money but, for peace of mind, it's normally worth every penny!

Points to consider

- How much is the deposit and when is it due?
- When is the balance due?
- Is VAT included in the final price?
- How far before the wedding must you order your dress?
- How many fittings will you need?
- Can you arrange at least one fitting with your bridal lingerie, shoes and other accessories?
- Confirm appointments for fittings and collection dates with a written contract.
- How far before the wedding can you expect your dress to arrive?
- What is the policy on cancellation/postponement?
- Have you insured the dress?
- If you hire your dress, check all the details before making your booking. Will your chosen dress be available on the day, cleaned and ready to collect? Does the hire cost cover the entire 24-hour period? Does the dress have to be cleaned before it is returned (this is very expensive)?

After the wedding

If you are buying or making a dress you may want to choose a style of dress that can be dyed or adapted for use as a black tie or cocktail dress afterwards. There are many firms that can provide such a service. If you wish to have your wedding dress dry-cleaned, do so within a few weeks of the wedding. Some firms sell special boxes to preserve your dress so that it will remain in pristine condition for years.

Choosing accessories

Depending on the style of dress you choose, you'll also have to make decisions on a whole host of accessories.

Veils and headdresses

Wedding veils are generally made of lace or tulle and secured by a circlet of flowers or a tiara. The general rule is that the more formal the dress, the longer the veil. You also need to think about how your veil will be held in place.

Veils and tiaras are often treasured in families and worn by generations of brides, so you might be able to borrow one or both from your own family or the groom's. Make sure you practise putting on your veil at least a week before the wedding, and don't leave it till the last minute on the actual day.

You could have a headdress made up with real flowers – usually the same varieties as in your bouquet – which should be made up and delivered on the day by the same florist. Most florists offering a bridal service will have several designs of headdresses from which to choose.

Fabric flowers may prove less of a worry, as obviously they will remain in perfect condition throughout the day. Bridal shops and stores have a wide range to choose from.

Try on a selection of headdresses before buying one, preferably with your dress on. You may prefer to wear a hat to complete your outfit, particularly if your dress is not a traditional wedding dress.

Lingerie

When it comes to lingerie, you will need to try everything on with your dress in order to check that there are no lines showing or straps peeping out! Remember that, although you want to feel glamorous on your wedding day, you want to feel like you. If you are simply not a stockings and suspenders person, don't torture yourself by wearing them on the day.

Shoes

Shoes are the most important accessories. They need to be comfortable, non-slip and with a heel to complement both your height and the dress. The sooner you find your perfect pair the better! Take them with you to dress fittings. On the day, don't forget to have a spare pair of stockings or tights to hand for those inevitable ladders. Wear your shoes around the house before the wedding to wear them in – trying to look serene and beautiful is not easy when that blister on your heel is getting bigger by the minute! If you're scared of getting ivory satin shoes dirty before your wedding, put a pair of clean pop socks over them for protection.

Gloves

If you're wearing gloves, the ring finger on the left hand must be exposed for the exchange of rings. This is accomplished by simply cutting along the base where the finger joins the main body of the glove. Some gloves are available 'ready-ripped'.

Wedding outfits

The groom's attire

A wedding is a chance for men – as well as women – to dress up. Tradition dictates that the groom, best man, ushers, father of the bride and groom's father should all look similar – if the groom is wearing morning dress, other men in the party should too – and the bride will often have strong preferences about what she wants the men to wear.

The important thing at any event, and especially at your wedding, is to feel at ease. If more formal dressing makes the groom feel uncomfortable, then lounge suits are a good alternative. This is definitely a sharp and sophisticated choice, and while associated with register office weddings, is perfectly acceptable for religious weddings as well.

Should the bride be keen on creating a coordinated look, the groom can mix a lounge suit with any shirt and tie, which can easily be matched or contrasted with the wedding colour theme.

Whatever look you go for, the men need to kit themselves out from top to toe for the best day ever.

Traditional men's wedding attire

Morning suit This is a combination of penguin dress coat, top hat and tails. The outfit is worn with a white wing-collar shirt, a waistcoat of any colour, a cravat, a top hat and a pair of gloves (just held, not worn).

Black tie (aka dinner suit) This is a black dinner jacket, either single- or double-breasted and tapered trousers. The evening shirt, in cotton or silk, with either a Marcella or pleated front, has a soft, turn-down collar and your bow tie should be black silk.

White tie A white-tie event is the most formal of all occasions. You need to wear a black evening tail coat with silk facings, black dress trousers with a white Marcella waistcoat, a dress shirt and bow tie.

Alternative wedding menswear may include frock coats, kilts or simply smart suits. The main thing is to be comfortable and confident in what you're wearing.

The bride's going-away outfit

Like her wedding dress, the bride's going-away outfit is often a source of great public interest. An elegant dress or suit is often chosen for town weddings. For a country wedding, the outfit can be more casual. However, you may like to consider changing out of your dress earlier at the reception so you can strut your stuff unimpeded on the dance floor! Remember that it is not obligatory to have a going-away outfit.

Pregnant brides

One London wedding dress store recently estimated that up to 20 per cent of its customers were expecting. But none of the major stores carries specific maternity lines. Although they may not overly advertise the fact, wedding dress suppliers do stress that they will try to ensure that the pregnant bride won't miss out on the dress of her dreams.

Etiquette corner: Something old, something new, something borrowed and something blue This tradition apparently brings all the available mystical influences into the bride's possession! Something old is the past, something new the future, and something borrowed the present. Something blue symbolizes purity. In addition, carrying a lucky charm, such as a silver horseshoe, is still a popular thing to do.

The bridesmaids

It's usual for the bride to choose the bridesmaids' outfits. Traditionally, these are paid for by the bridesmaids themselves for the privilege of taking part. Nowadays, payment is either shared or negotiated – but discuss this up front. Once you add up the cost of the material, shoes, dressmaking and accessories, it can be an expensive business!

Choosing their dresses

The bride's choice of bridesmaids' dresses will depend on several factors, most importantly what she is wearing herself. If she chooses a long elaborate gown, then her bridesmaids can be similarly attired. If, however, she decides to marry in a shorter, simpler style, then it would look odd for the attendants to be dressed in frills and flounces.

If the bridesmaids are of varying shapes and sizes, you have the complicated task of choosing a style and colour to suit them all. One solution is for you to choose material of a certain shade and for the bridesmaids to have dresses made in that same shade and in a style that suits them. Once the style and fabric have been chosen, your chief bridesmaid should coordinate the other bridesmaids' fitting sessions, to take the pressure off you.

If lots of money is being spent on the dresses, it's wise to get something that can be worn again, to a ball or a smart dinner, or you may want to sell them after the wedding.

Making the bridesmaids' dresses is a much more popular option than making your own dress because they are often simpler in design and decoration, and they can be made at home more easily.

Accessories

Bridesmaids often wear headdresses and usually carry flowers. Colour and style are important here, as a certain style of headdress may not suit all age groups and individual face shapes and colourings.

Shoes are generally formal, matching coloured or light court shoes or sandals for the adults, with soft shoes, such as ballet pumps, for the young ones.

Bridesmaids carry bouquets, posies or flower baskets. Again, the colours of the chosen flowers should enhance the bride's chosen colour scheme.

Flower girls and page-boys

The job of these junior helpers is chiefly to take part in the bridal procession to and from the marriage venue, looking as sweet and endearing as possible.

Flower girls generally wear a mini version of either the bride's dress or the bridesmaids' dresses. Usually, they carry a posy or a basket of flowers or petals, which they strew up the aisle in front of the bride. However, some ministers don't appreciate this, so get permission first!

Page-boys are often dressed in sailor suits, or Little Lord Fauntleroy outfits. Usually, you can get only a very young boy to agree to this kind of outfit without a fight!

Alternatives are to dress the page-boys in smart trousers and waistcoats, or even in a slightly less overwhelming kind of morning dress (if that's what the ushers are wearing). They do not carry flowers.

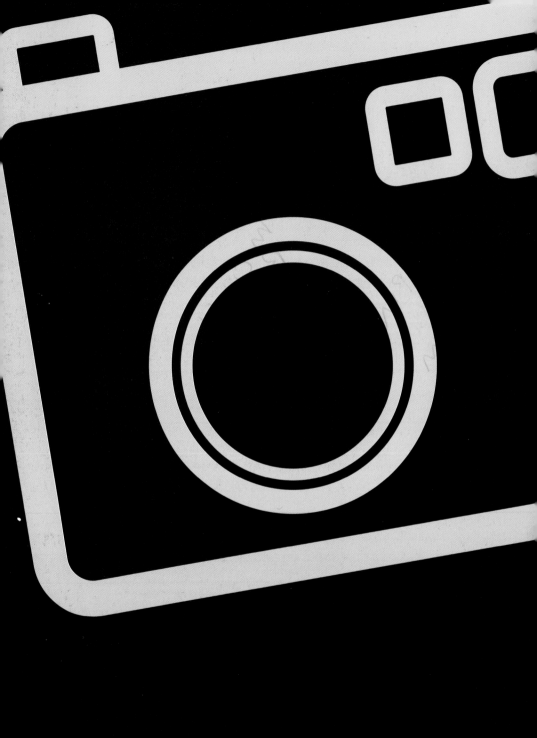

Transport,
flowers and
photography

Transport

The journey to your wedding venue may be one of the most nerve-wracking and emotional of your life, and the trip to your reception may be the most wonderful, so there's every reason to do both in style and/or comfort. Push the boat out – literally, if you want to!

The style of your wedding will dictate the type of transport you choose, but keep in mind that anything fancy will come with a fancy price tag. Besides your budget, you'll need to consider practical issues carefully. Arriving by hot-air balloon is not the ideal time to discover your paralyzing fear of heights.

Before deciding on your mode of transport, consider the style of your wedding, distances involved, time of journey and time of year. For example, a horse-drawn carriage is romantic, but inappropriate for a long journey in winter. One last thing: make sure that your groom doesn't make arrangements for something unusual without consulting you.

Transport options

Although a vintage Rolls or Daimler is the traditional and
certainly the most glamorous way to arrive at your wedding,
there are some weird and wonderful alternatives!

Classy motor

A stretch limousine adds a dash of Hollywood glamour to
the proceedings and you'll feel like a star. Alternatively, plump
for a classic American car like a 1950s Cadillac in a funky
colour like bubblegum pink! If the pair of you are sports-car
fanatics, why not hire a spectacular set of wheels and roll up
in a racy Ferrari, Porsche, Aston Martin – or even matching
Mini Coopers à la *The Italian Job*?

My little pony (and trap)

Fulfil your fantasies of the perfect fairy-tale wedding by
drawing up in a horse and carriage. Intensely romantic and
very picturesque, this mode of transport is perfect for a
country wedding where you won't have to negotiate busy roads.

Chopper's away

For an entrance worthy of a Bond girl, arrive by helicopter.
This is not only a thrilling way to travel, but it can also be
very practical, especially if your ceremony venue is some way
from your home or the reception. But this is one to avoid if
you're a nervous flyer, worried about crushing your dress or
messing up your hair, or on a tight budget!

On foot

If you live very close to the venue of your ceremony, why not
walk there?

Drive your own

If you're passionate about your own car, why not use it on the big day?

Water berth

For a wedding in a riverside hotel, arrive by boat.

Marriage à la Mod

If you're marrying abroad, say on a Greek island, zip into your ceremony on Vespa scooters, hired locally.

Cabbing it

A white Hackney cab is an inexpensive, practical and very stylish way to be transported to your wedding.

Something on the side

For a cute and quirky means of transport, try a vintage motorbike and sidecar.

Transport checklist

- Which journeys will you need transport for?
- How will the groom, best man and members of the wedding party travel to the ceremony?
- Is transport required for guests?
- Choose transport that's in keeping with the style of your wedding.
- Make sure you see the vehicle before booking or paying a deposit – photos and leaflets don't show marks, dents or a scruffy interior.
- How much does the company charge? Is there a minimum charge?

- Is a standard wedding package offered? Is there a discount when booking extra vehicles?
- Are decorations and champagne included? Can these be left out in exchange for an upgraded vehicle?
- Are the drivers/operators certified?
- What will they wear?
- What kind of licensing/insurance do they have?
- What is the contingency plan should your vehicle not be available on the day?
- How far in advance will you have to make your booking?
- What is the company's policy on cancellation/postponement?
- How much is the deposit to secure the date and when is it due?
- When is the balance due?
- Is VAT included in the final price?
- Confirm dates, times and locations with a written contract, and reconfirm any bookings that you have made the week before the wedding.
- Get insurance.
- Choose a wedding car in a colour that doesn't clash with the bride's bouquet or the bridesmaids' dresses.

  - Buy the ribbon for the car in advance and ask a reliable (and handy) member of the bridal party to attach it on the day. This can be fiddly to do, so practice is essential.
  - Colour coordinate the car ribbon with your flowers and/or the colour theme of your wedding.
  - If you're using your own car or borrowing one, have it valeted – you don't want to have to scramble over empty crisp packets or end up sitting on the dog's blanket!
  - Make sure you can easily enter/exit the vehicle in your dress.
  - Have a bottle of champagne chilling on ice in the back of the vehicle for a post-ceremony celebratory drink.

Wedding flowers

Deciding on the flowers for your wedding needs to be done at about the same time as you arrange your transport – well in advance and at least six months before the wedding. Choose varieties to complement the style of your day, and enlist the help of someone who knows what they're doing.

Make sure that you allow enough money to pay for all the flowers you want. Do your research thoroughly – you'll probably be very surprised at how much flowers cost!

Normally, the groom pays for the bride's bouquet, buttonholes, corsages and the flowers for the bridesmaids, while the bride's parents pay for the ceremony and reception flowers. Remember to get a written quotation from your florist well in advance and make sure that it covers all the extras, including floral headdresses, and thank-you bouquets for the mothers, if you're having them.

Whatever flowers you decide on, keep your arrangements to scale with the venue and occasion. A grand wedding requires more stylized floral arrangements, while a small reception at home could be adequately catered for with simple vase arrangements and bunches of flowers.

Flowers for the wedding party
The bride usually carries a bouquet and wears flowers in her hair or a 'crown' of flowers to hold her veil in place. Be careful when choosing flowers for buttonholes, corsages and hair. They should be wired or preserved, or they may wilt before the day is out.

The bride's flowers set the tone and scheme for the bridesmaids' bouquets, the buttonholes for the groom, best man, ushers and father of the bride, and the corsages for the couple's mothers. The tradition of a flower girl strewing petals along the aisle of the church for the bride to step on dates from the Middle Ages. Very sweet, but check first that your officiant approves!

Finding a florist

You need to decide whether to employ a professional florist or get family or a friend to do some floral DIY. Don't forget that most of the arranging will need to be done immediately before the wedding – a time when things are at their most hectic – so don't rope in a key member of the bridal party. They won't thank you for it!

If you don't already have a florist in mind, by far the best method for choosing one is by recommendation. Standards of service vary considerably. Always ask to see photos of other wedding flower arrangements that the florist has done.

The price of flowers can be alarming and much depends on seasonal availability, so to cut costs find out what's in season (see page 107) and work round it. When visiting a florist, take as much information with you as possible to help them to help you. If possible, take sketches of your dress, the attendants' clothes and samples of the fabrics. You could also cut out pictures of the kinds of bouquet you particularly like. All this will help the florist achieve the best possible result for your special day. A good florist will ask to visit the church or register office and the reception venue if you've hired them to decorate those as well.

Flowers for each event

Church flowers

The most usual positions for flower arrangements are on the chancel steps, the windowsills and the pew-ends. Some clergymen will allow the altar to be decorated; others are strongly opposed to the idea.

Your celebrant may suggest that the floral decorations be left to those who arrange the church flowers every week. The advantage of this is that they know where flowers show to the best advantage. However, if you're not happy with this arrangement, tactfully negotiate – after all, you'll be paying for the flowers and possibly the arranger, too!

Find out if another wedding service is taking place on the same day as yours. If so, it makes sense for the brides to make contact with each other and perhaps arrange to share the cost. You could always ask for your flowers to be given to a local hospital or old people's home after the ceremony (and usually after the Sunday service is over).

Register office flowers

Many register offices change their flowers every day. However, you may be allowed to bring in a special arrangement, if you wish.

Reception flowers

Flower arrangements are very much determined by the venue and the kind of reception you are having. It's nice for guests waiting in line to see an arrangement of flowers nearby. Other arrangements can be placed around the hall or

Matching the season

These days you can find almost any kind of flower at any time of the year, but you may prefer something to suit the season of your wedding.

Spring Daffodils, narcissi, bluebells, freesias, tulips, hyacinths.

Summer Roses, hydrangeas, stephanotis, lisianthus, sunflowers, sweet peas, delphiniums, larkspur.

Autumn Chrysanthemums, wheat, euphorbia, hypericum berries, alstromeria, gerbera.

Winter Ivy, lilies, orchids, hippeastrum, dark red roses, dendrobium.

marquee. Smaller displays on individual tables add an air of festivity and charm.

If a hall or rooms are being hired for the reception, flowers are sometimes included in the package. Make sure they will be to your liking and match your colour scheme. Again, you might be able to share the costs with a bride who is holding a reception there the day before or after yours.

Many couples prefer to use fresh flowers to adorn their wedding cake rather than artificial ones.

The bouquet

Most brides like to include their favourite flowers in their bouquet, but the style of the wedding dress and colours of the wedding party are the most important aspects to be considered.

There are many different types of bridal bouquet, from a wild flower posy to a basket of flowers, a single amazing lily stem or a traditional sheaf of varied blooms. Some brides even choose a freeze-dried bouquet, which lasts forever. There are many companies who will preserve your fresh flower bouquet, too.

Finding the right photographer

Start your search for a photographer early because good ones get booked up a long time in advance. And before you make your final choice, try to visit at least three photographers – check out their studio and staff and don't be afraid to ask questions. Ask to see full wedding album samples and make sure that the photos you're shown are the work of the person who will be taking your wedding pictures, not simply the best photos from the studio.

It's important to check credentials. Check if the photographer is a qualified member of MPA (Master Photographers Association), BIPP (British Institute of Professional Photographers) or Guild of Wedding Photographers.

Whoever you book to take your pictures will be spending a substantial amount of time with you on the best day of your lives, so you must get on with him or her and feel confident and relaxed in their presence. If you don't feel comfortable, this will be reflected in the final images.

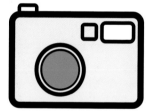

Is the price right?

Prices range from anything upwards of £500, and wedding photography is one area where you really do get what you pay for. Most photographers have a menu of prices and will charge you a flat rate for taking shots on the day, plus an additional charge based on how many photographs you want in your album.

The quality of the albums on offer (leather, plastic, velvet) can vary enormously and this will affect the cost as well. Remember that your family will be charged separately for any copies they want. Look for those nice little extras, though – some photographers will include thank-you cards with a small photo enclosed as part of the deal.

Photography checklist

- Once you've found the right photographer and decided on a style, get your booking in writing.
- Check the small print and make sure you know exactly what you're getting for your money.
- Ask the photographer to sign a contract that records your wedding date, time and place, price and any restrictions or conditions.
- Ascertain when the proofs will be ready and how long you can keep them to make your selection.
- Find out exactly when your album will be ready, too.

Think style and colour

There are lots of ways for your photographer to record your wedding, from the traditional posed group shots to more candid reportage-style shots, such as the bride in her curlers. Most couples choose a combination of styles and film.

If you want a complete formal record of the whole wedding, it's best to go for traditional photographs. Couples seeking a more relaxed, unposed album, on the other hand, should choose reportage style. If you've spent a long time creating invitations, menus, flower arrangements and the like, you'll want a photographer who will capture these little details on film, too.

You'll need to decide whether to go for black-and-white or colour photographs. Couples who have carefully colour coordinated their day will want photos that record their creation. Black-and-white, meanwhile, creates a more timeless image. Some photographers will agree to do a combination.

Many couples place disposable cameras on the tables at the reception for guests to take their own pictures of the celebrations. Ask guests to leave the cameras behind at the end of the evening for you to develop the films. The photos will give you a unique insight into your day from other people's points of view!

Planning for the perfect pictures

Try to meet up at the venues for the service and the reception beforehand, so that the photographer can get a feel for the best settings to enhance the style of photographs. Remember that you need to check with your minister to make sure photography is permitted during the wedding ceremony.

A good professional photographer will use his or her creative and technical skills to get the best results as quickly, smoothly and tactfully as possible, but discuss the role you want your photographer to undertake on your wedding day. Do you want him or her to control events or blend into the background? One well-known photographer likes to shepherd guests into position with the help of a shrill whistle. It's not very subtle, but it breaks the ice and no one misses out on any of the photo calls.

If you are not used to posing, or feel unhappy with your usual image in pictures, spend some time before your big day practising until you find a smile or expression you can live with. If you look and feel comfortable, your photos are bound to work!

Remember to stand up straight, with your head back, no double chins, and smile – a lot of people will be taking photographs of you and you'll want them to catch you at your best.

The shoot list
Before the big day, discuss a rough shoot list with your photographer. The traditional choices include:
- groom and best man outside the church/civil venue
- bride's arrival at the church/civil venue
- bride and father walking down the aisle/bride entering the civil venue
- bride and groom at the altar/desk
- exchange of rings
- signing of the church register/documentation
- procession out of the church/civil venue
- group shots outside the church/civil venue
- arriving at the reception
- cutting the cake

Video star!

Using a professional

For a slick and infinitely watchable video, you generally need to hire a professional videomaker. However, be warned: the cost can be prohibitive.

The best way to find a videomaker is through recommendation. Alternatively, contact the Association of Professional Videomakers. Always ask to see samples of their work and watch a video of a whole wedding, not a tape of edited highlights. Make sure the same person who filmed the wedding you are watching will film your wedding.

Book your videomaker well in advance. Next determine exactly what is included in the price and whether there will be extra charges for editing, adding titles and dubbing music, and whether you can choose your own music. Let the videomaker know if there are specific moments or people you want included in the video.

Using an amateur

If your budget won't stretch to hiring a professional, ask a friend or relative to video the big day for you. An amateur video will never be as perfect as a professionally made one, but it can still capture all the joy of the day.

Get your appointed 'cameraman' to experiment with the camera well in advance and plan what is to be filmed. Make sure they use a tripod for the ceremony as the footage will be steadier, and they don't rapidly zoom in or out or the images will be blurred. Remember too much footage is better than too little – the video can always be edited down.

Photography and video checklist

- Is the photographer/videomaker available before and after the ceremony, at your home and at the reception?
- How do they charge? Flat fee? By the hour?
- What kind of packages do they offer? Can you make substitutions?
- Are prints/extra videotapes included in the price? Is the cost of an album included in the price?
- Are they willing to follow a list of requested shots?
- Will they have an assistant/assistants? Is their cost included in the price?
- What will everyone be wearing?
- Are you expected to provide food and/or transportation?
- If there is an emergency, will you be sent an alternative photographer/videomaker? If yes, can you see examples of their work?
- How soon after the wedding will the proofs/tapes be available? How long can you have the proofs before you make your selection?
- How long will the photographer keep the negatives?
- Who owns the rights to the images?
- How far in advance are bookings required?
- What is their policy on cancellation/postponement?
- How much is the deposit to secure the date?
- When is the deposit due?
- How soon after the event is the balance due?
- Is VAT included in the final price?
- Confirm dates, times and locations with a written contract.
- Get insurance.

The
reception

The reception

Planning for the reception should begin as soon as you set the wedding date – usually at least three months in advance. Popular venues (or any venue on popular dates like a bank holiday) may need to be reserved up to one year before the event, so get a provisional booking in as soon as you can.

It's important that you celebrate your marriage in a style to suit you, so don't feel forced into the conventional sit-down meal in a marquee if you'd rather eat fish and chips in your local pub.

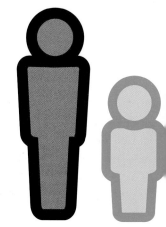

Who does what?

The bride's family is traditionally responsible for making all the reception arrangements and absorbing the cost, which can mean paying for food, drink, a wedding cake, caterers, waiting staff, a toastmaster, flower arrangements, a band or disco, entertainers or musicians and any security arrangements. Sometimes couples cover the cost of the wedding reception themselves or share it between the families. Whoever's footing the bill, it's the reception that is likely to be the single biggest expense of the wedding, so plan it carefully.

When to have your reception

The timing of your reception is really up to you. You can have a wedding breakfast, which is the traditional name for what is actually a sit-down lunch following a morning wedding ceremony. Or you can have an afternoon reception, held after a 2.30 or 3pm service. This is usually followed by an evening party/disco held some hours later, which gives everybody time to change into less formal clothes, if they wish. However, make sure that your guests, particularly those from out of town, are not left stranded with nothing to do between the end of the lunch and the beginning of the evening celebrations.

Sometimes the 'evening do' is hosted by the couple themselves and invitations are issued in their names. This is also a chance to invite people you couldn't afford to feed! The more continental late-afternoon service, followed by an evening reception with dinner and dancing, has recently become quite fashionable. Guests are invited to wear evening dress to the ceremony. If you're getting married abroad in a hot climate, a late afternoon or early morning ceremony is best, unless you want to fry!

You might find your reception timetable is partly dictated by licensing laws. You need to check how late a venue's licence extends before you make a firm booking. Even if your reception is in a hotel, where overnight guests can continue to purchase drinks legally, there may be a limit on how long the music is allowed to go on.

Choosing the venue

When women used to live at home until they were married, wedding receptions were traditionally held at the bride's family home. Today, receptions can take place almost anywhere – hotels, banqueting halls, clubs, marquees, a village hall or stately home.

The number of people you want at your reception may well dictate your choice of venue – or vice versa! It is usual for everyone who has been invited to the wedding ceremony to be asked to the reception. If only a small number of guests can attend the ceremony due to lack of space, or you want a very private ceremony, then additional guests can be invited to the reception afterwards. For 100 guests or more, consider rooms designed specifically for holding receptions, as they will have all the facilities you need.

Your venue is the place where you are going to entertain all of your friends and relations – so take your time to get it right. Start your search a long time – ideally a year – before your party as this gives you time to make the right decision without rushing into anything.

Services and cost

Most reception venues will quote you a cost per head for food and drink, a hire charge for the venue (or marquee) plus the cost of any entertainment, a toastmaster, cake stand, and so on.

In your initial consultation with a venue, get a full list of all the possible costs and charges. Decide roughly what your budget is and your ideal head count and then the venue price range will become clear. A venue will be able to offer you a number of services, which may include a registrar, food, drink and music as well as accommodation. Many will take a lot of the organization out of your hands and will employ a wedding coordinator or events manager.

Somewhere unique

There are lots of exciting venues that have civil wedding licences, so not only can you have your reception somewhere really different – you can get married there too. How about:

A castle Romantic piles all over the UK are available for wedding and reception hire. Perfect for a medieval themed wedding.

A museum You can have your reception at London's Natural History Museum and lots of local museums also cater for weddings, with some having civil wedding licences.

The London Eye Get married with the city spread out before you. You'll be pronounced man and wife when the big wheel gets to the top, and served champagne on the way down.

The zoo Edinburgh Zoo and London Zoo host weddings and receptions.

Somewhere sporty Try a racecourse, golf club or any sporting venue that's close to your heart.

Think laterally. You may have seen a building or even a private house that you feel would be perfect. Although some places look as if they may be unavailable, don't believe it until you have asked.

Hiring a marquee

A marquee is a good option for large gatherings, and you may like to set one up in your own garden or that of willing parents or a friend. Marquees are no longer simply poled tents. Nowadays, they are framed structures that don't need ropes or poles, and the space within the marquee is clear.

Marquees come in a huge array of shapes, sizes, prices and specifications. Do shop around and find out what is available for the date you have chosen. Remember that your marquee will need flooring and a lining as well as other components that are costed separately, for example, lighting, heating and furniture – so you'll need to take these costs into consideration. Ask to see samples of fabrics used for the marquee lining – the wide choice of linings available means that you can choose colours that will complement your theme. Because heated marquees are now available you should be cosy, whatever the weather!

Before booking your marquee it is a good idea to show the hire company the site to ensure that it's suitable for your requirements.

Marquee checklist

- Is the location close enough to the place of worship or register office?
- Will holding the reception at home increase the stress factor dramatically?
- Are lavatory and cloakroom facilities sufficient?
- Can the hire company arrange for portable toilets, if necessary?

- Will the caterers be able to function in the kitchen of the home or will you need to hire a portable kitchen?
- Is there space for a bar?
- Is there sufficient parking space?
- Will the company do an on-site estimate?
- Will a marquee accommodate all your guests? Is there room to mingle? Is there room for a dance floor?
- What colour is the marquee? What types of lining are available?
- Is proper flooring available? What about staging for the speeches and entertainment?
- Is the hire of tables and chairs included in the price?
- Is there a sufficient power supply for any entertainment/ sound systems you may require? Can the hire company provide a generator if additional electricity is needed?
- Can they provide interior lighting? Exterior lighting? Heating? A public address system for speeches?

- Can your theme and decorations be incorporated into the structure easily?
- Is access to permanent shelter/house available?
- Can walkways be covered?
- When will the marquee need to be set up and dismantled?
- Will someone be available on-call during the event if there are any emergencies?
- How far in advance are bookings required?
- What is the policy on cancellation/postponement?
- How much is the deposit to secure the date? When is it due?
- How soon after the event is the balance due?
- Is VAT included in the final price?
- Confirm dates, times and details with a written contract.
- Get insurance.

Venue checklist

This sounds like an off-beat tip... but it's probably the most significant of all. You need to establish early on whether or not the management of your venue is on your side or not. Most are friendly and flexible, but there are certain museums and historic buildings run by managers/caretakers who are, deep down, 'anti-party' people – they would prefer to see their venues full of art or exhibits instead of wine and music.

Venue checklist

- Is the venue big enough to accommodate all your guests?
- Is the reception venue within a reasonable distance of the ceremony venue? How easy is it to find? Is it well sign-posted?
- Are there adequate parking facilities?
- Is there accommodation at the venue?
- What types of wedding package are available?
- Does the venue have an in-house wedding coordinator?
- Are there any special conditions imposed by the venue?
- Are there adequate cloakroom and lavatory facilities?
- Are there facilities and special seating for less mobile guests or anyone with a disability?
- Are there any special facilities for children?
- Does the venue have equipment you can use? Will you have to hire tables, chairs, linen, crockery, cutlery, glassware?
- Are the tables, chairs, linen and overall ambience appropriate for your style of wedding?
- Are decorations, such as flowers, included?
- Can you bring in your own choice of caterer, florist, decorator and other services?

- If you are bringing in a caterer, will they have access to a kitchen, power supply and running water?
- Can the venue supply the cake stand and knife?
- Does the venue have a licence to consume alcohol? Is there a late-night curfew? Until what time will the bar be open?
- Can you supply your own alcohol? Is there a corkage fee?
- How will the staff be dressed? How many will be required?
- Is a toastmaster included in the staffing costs?
- Is entertainment permitted?
- Is smoking permitted?

- Is there a sufficient power supply for any entertainment/sound systems you may require?
- Is there a public address system for speeches?
- Are there noise level restrictions?
- Is the lighting suitable?
- Where can guests store coats and personal belongings?
- Is there a safe place for storing gifts?
- Are there other weddings booked for the same day?
- When will you be allowed access to the venue?
- Is there a private room in which you can change into going-away outfits?
- Can you see the room while it's being used for another wedding reception?
- Does the venue have public liability insurance?
- How far in advance are bookings required?
- What is the policy on cancellation/postponement?
- How much is the deposit and when is it due?
- How soon after the event is the balance due?
- Is VAT included in the final price?
- Confirm dates, times and details with a written contract.
- Get insurance.

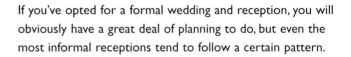

At the reception

If you've opted for a formal wedding and reception, you will obviously have a great deal of planning to do, but even the most informal receptions tend to follow a certain pattern.

The receiving line

A traditional formal receiving line is where the bride and groom line up with both sets of parents and greet each guest as they enter the room. It is advisable to go through the guest list together before the day, so that everyone is acquainted with the guests' names.

The receiving line can be as the guests leave the wedding ceremony or as they arrive at the reception, which is the most popular choice. If you have a master of ceremonies, they can announce each guest as they enter the room.

What are the options?

- The conventional line, based on the notion that the bride's parents are paying for the entire wedding, is to have the bride's mother and father first, then the groom's parents and then the bride and groom. You may also like to add the best man and chief bridesmaid to the end of the line.
- For a smaller line, you and the groom may prefer to greet the guests on your own.
- Alternatively, you may not want to have a receiving line at all. This is your choice, but remember that it does give you the chance to talk to every guest individually at least once on the day and thank them for coming.

Seating plans

The seating plan for the meal is based on the idea of intermingling the two families, but many people organize their seating plans so that guests have familiar faces around them.

Sorting out the seating plan is not an easy task. Tact and a good knowledge of the guests are vital. It is also worth remembering that weddings can be a reunion for friends and relatives who normally do not have an opportunity to meet. It's also where old enemies may come face to face again!

The layout of your tables is a personal choice. Some like the idea of an elongated top table, where extensions are added at right angles to both ends of the top table. Guests can be seated on both sides of these side tables. Alternatively, individual round tables can be arranged for the guests.

No matter how hard you try, you might end up with a seating plan with tables of people who've never met before. If you're worried that your tables are too 'mixed' and you need an icebreaker, why not place quizzes about the bride and groom on all the tables?

You should discuss the layout of the tables with the hotel staff or catering firm and agree the seating plan well in advance. On the day, the seating plan can be placed on an easel for the guests to see as they come in for the meal, and there should be corresponding place cards on the tables. If you have a lot of guests, set up several easels so that everyone can check their seat number easily without causing a crowd to build up.

The top table

The traditional top table for the wedding party has everyone seated down one side of a rectangular table, facing the rest of the room. The usual arrangement is, from the left: chief bridesmaid, groom's father, bride's mother, groom, bride, bride's father, groom's mother, best man (see below).

An alternative to this is to swap the fathers so that the bride's parents sit together and the groom's parents sit together. Whether you split the parents and put them with each other's partner or not is up to you. It's less and less common to have a formal seating arrangement on the top table, so go with what will make everyone happiest.

Remember that the top table is always the focus of attention, and any resentment or bitterness lurking between people, for example, current partners and exes, is going to be very obvious.

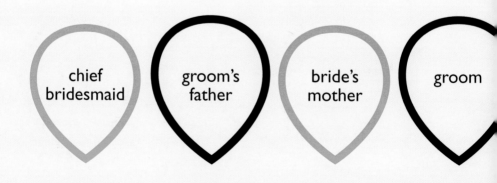

chief bridesmaid | groom's father | bride's mother | groom

If you have large numbers of extended family, you might need to be a little more creative with your 'top table' arrangement. A round (non-hierarchical) table is always a good way to solve this problem. But who says all the leading players in your wedding have to sit together anyway? You could set up several tables, rather than just the one top table.

While it's best to avoid seating sworn enemies next to each other, sometimes it's unavoidable. If this happens, warn each person in advance and trust that their love for you will take precedence over their mutual animosity. It's important to remember that the onus is on others to cooperate and be at least civil to one another. It's not for you to come up with the seating plan from heaven that will magically wipe out all tension. Of course you want people to get on and be happy on your special day, but don't let their issues become yours.

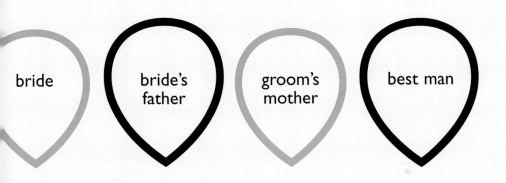

Reception traditions

It's your wedding day, and it's up to you how your reception runs. But if you want to stick to a traditional way of doing things, there are some key elements that you won't want to miss out.

As well as the receiving line and the top table, wedding receptions have traditions for opening the dancing, cutting the cake, giving gifts, going home and disposing of the bouquet. Then, of course, there are the speeches...

Speeches and toasts

Most receptions include speeches and toasts. These should always be properly planned, rehearsed and timed. Usually they come at the end of the meal, although there is an increasing trend to have them before the meal begins. Usually, the father of the bride speaks first and then toasts the bride and groom. Next comes the groom – and perhaps the bride. They thank their guests for coming and, traditionally, the groom proposes a toast to the bridesmaids. Then, finally, comes the best man, who officially 'replies' on behalf of the bridesmaids.

Favours

It's usual nowadays to give each guest a tiny gift, or favour, to remind them of the wedding day. These range from traditional Italian sugared almonds, more modern confectionery options, such as chocolates or jelly beans, to perfumed candles, even extravagant silver trinkets.

Cutting the cake

The bride and groom cut the cake together as a symbol of their shared future. After the cake-cutting ceremony (usually at the very end of the meal and after the speeches), the caterers remove the cake, which is sliced up and handed round to guests.

First dance

Traditionally, the bride and groom have the 'first dance' together. This would have been a waltz in the past, but nowadays it's whatever you choose. If you don't relish the idea of dancing in public, open the dance floor to everyone as soon as the music starts.

It is also traditional for the groom to dance with his new mother-in-law and then with his mother, while the bride dances with her new father-in-law and then her father. The best man joins in by dancing with the chief bridesmaid, while the ushers dance with the other bridesmaids.

Timely departure

Guests are supposed to remain at the reception until the couple leave, so if there is to be no formal 'going away', let your guests know (especially the older ones) that you intend to dance the night away!

Tossing the bouquet

After the reception, the bride throws her bouquet over her shoulder towards a group of her unmarried girlfriends and female relatives. Traditionally, the one who catches the flowers (and survives the scrum!) will be the next to marry.

Entertainment

The entertainment you have at your wedding offers an unrivalled opportunity for flights of fancy and extravagance. On the other hand, you can keep it simple and affordable. At your daytime reception, you could hire, say, a harpist and flute duo, a string quartet or a small jazz band to make some pretty background noise. Their repertoire should be light enough to appeal to a varied age group and never so loud that it overwhelms the conversation.

The evening entertainment is a matter of personal choice. Anything goes, from karaoke to a live orchestra, from a jazz band to a raging disco. Just bear in mind the age range of your guests and the layout of the venue.

From ceilidhs to discos, the entertainment is a vital part of the celebrations and often takes up a big part of the evening. Ensure that you have heard or seen any entertainers. Bands might send tapes or invitations to hear them play, and DJs should allow you to choose many or all of the songs played. Alternatively, entertainment agents can arrange everything for you. Reputable agents should be registered with either The Entertainment Agents Association of Great Britain or The National Entertainment Agents Council. You might want to consider alternative entertainment, such as magicians, casino games and fireworks.

Entertainment checklist

- What type of entertainment would you like? DJ? Dance band? Cover band?
- How do they charge? Do they offer any special packages or discounts? Is there a minimum time requirement? Will they play overtime and at what cost? Are travel costs included?
- Will you be responsible for feeding the entertainers?
- Do they have a demo tape you can listen to?
- Where can you hear them perform live?
- In the case of a band, how long have these particular musicians been playing together and performing at weddings?
- What time will they arrive? How long will it take to set up?
- How often do they take breaks and how long are they?
- Can arrangements be made for taped music to be played during breaks?

- What will they be wearing?
- Does the venue have an entertainment licence?
- Can the volume be easily controlled?
- Does the DJ work from a predetermined playlist?
- Are you able to pass on a list of songs you do or don't want?
- Are they able to accommodate requests?
- Is there any equipment you will need to supply?
- How far in advance are bookings required?
- What is the policy on cancellation/postponement?
- How much is the deposit to secure the date and when is it due?
- How soon after the event is the balance due?
- Is VAT included in the final price?
- Confirm dates, times and details with a written contract.
- Get insurance.

Food and drink

Once you've found your ideal venue, you and your fiancé and/or your parents should make an appointment with the person in charge to discuss dates, times, numbers of guests, the catering and the exact price of everything.

The catering and refreshments will very much depend on the venue and type of reception you have decided to organize. Some venues may have resident caterers, others may be able to recommend caterers or may even insist that you use a particular one. However, for a low-key affair, local restaurants, bakers, off-licences and even supermarkets will be more than willing to give you an estimate. Seriously consider a professional caterer if your guest list exceeds 20, then you won't have to worry about dirty dishes and whether or not everyone has had enough to eat. Hire staff to serve and clear up – it's money well spent. It's probably best not to accept offers of help from invited guests – after all, they are meant to be celebrating with you!

Choosing a caterer

It is important to allow yourself sufficient time to get various estimates and to compare catering services, facilities and costs, if necessary. Remember that good caterers tend to get booked up months in advance.

A personal recommendation is always the best guide. If the caterer runs a restaurant or hotel, try to sample a meal before making your decision. Many hotels will let you sample their suggested wedding menus, either for free or at a reduced price, once you have made your booking with them.

Your caterer will need to know the date, time of reception, number of guests, level of hospitality you wish to provide and your limit on charges per head in order to supply you with ideas and quotations. Always ask for quotations and confirmation of everything in writing – and file your copies carefully!

And don't forget to finalize numbers with the caterers just before the wedding, especially if there are late cancellations, otherwise you'll have to pay for wasted meals.

Think about the style of reception you are having. A banquet caterer may not be appropriate for an intimate cocktail reception for 40 guests.

Menu options

You can have anything you like, from a light lunch to an elaborate dinner. After initial discussions and a briefing from you, a good caterer will suggest sample menus and help you with your decision.

• A finger buffet could include canapés, small sandwiches, individual pastries and dips. The guests do not require cutlery and are free to mingle and eat at the same time.

• A fork buffet can include a wide choice of food with a variety of salads and/or hot dishes. The guests serve themselves and then sit at specific places laid out for them on a seating plan.

• A sit-down meal is the traditional reception fare, but it is also the most expensive option. Usually there will be a minimum of three courses – starter, main course and dessert – plus coffee and cake.

Drinks for the wedding

The quantity and type of drinks provided will be determined both by the style of your meal and the number of guests. As well as alcoholic drinks, make sure there are plenty of non-alcoholic drinks, too, for children, drivers, older guests, those suffering from the heat and those suffering from perhaps too much champagne!

Drinks on arrival at the reception

It is normal to provide a drink for guests as they arrive at the reception. It may be an aperitif, like a medium or dry sherry, a glass of champagne or sparkling wine, or maybe buck's fizz or Pimms. There should also be a soft drink on offer, such as orange juice, especially if there are children at your wedding. For a winter wedding, mulled wine is a welcome option.

Drinks with the meal

At the meal itself, either champagne or sparkling wine can be served, but it is quite normal to have white or red wine, and often a bottle of each is placed on every table. Soft drinks should also be provided, such as orange juice or a more exotic non-alcoholic cocktail. It is also usual for bottles of water to be provided, possibly still and sparkling. If you're having an afternoon reception, you might also want to serve tea or coffee at some point.

Drinks for the toasts

It is traditional for a glass of champagne to be served to each guest prior to the speeches, so that they can toast the bride and groom. Alternatively, you could serve sparkling wine.

Drinks in the evening

If the celebrations go on into the evening, the hosts can arrange for drinks to be provided at their expense. It's quite acceptable to have a paying bar and for the bridal party to put some money behind it. Once that's been spent, guests pay for their own drinks.

Corkage

Your caterer or venue may provide the drinks, service and the necessary equipment, but do watch the price. Some venues allow the wedding organizer to provide the drink, but they tend to charge corkage, so you may not save much.

If you do arrange to buy drink from a supplier, such as an off-licence, make sure you get it on a sale-or-return basis. Usually suppliers can advise on the best choice of wines and provide glasses, ice buckets and ice.

Cake

Who will make the cake?

When ordering your cake, your options are:

- Buy a standard cake (and have it specially decorated).
- Have it made by a specialist.
- Have it made by a relative or friend and then iced professionally.
- Have it made and iced by a relative or friend.
- Order it from your local bakery.

You don't have to have a wedding cake at all, but it is traditional for the couple to formally 'cut' the cake while everyone looks on and cheers. In fact, it is an age-old symbol of fertility!

The traditional wedding cake is a rich fruit cake with thick icing. It's usually square or round and comes in two or three tiers. But there's nothing stopping you from choosing something completely different (see right).

Ordering your cake

Make sure that you order your wedding cake in good time – a multi-tiered cake can take months to create and it will need to be made and iced in different stages. Flowers generally form the main cake decorations (whether real, fabric or piped in icing), although some couples like to include balloons, ribbons or horseshoes and figurines.

It is best for the cake to be delivered to the reception venue unassembled and then the tiers put together in situ. Make sure your venue has somewhere safe to store the cake and that they can assemble it for you.

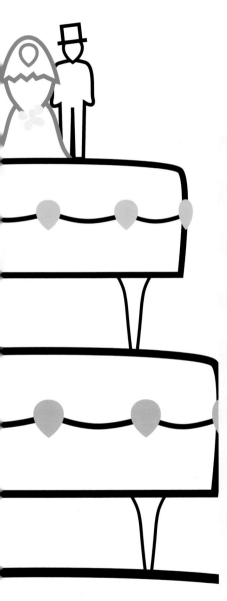

Bucking the trend

Don't fancy fruit cake? No problem. You don't have to have a traditional wedding cake at all. Here are a few alternatives:

- Try a wedding trifle – everyone loves the layers.
- Think old-fashioned tea party. Buy some interesting moulds and serve up platefuls of jelly and ice cream.
- What about a *croquembouche*? This traditional French wedding cake is made from profiteroles and glazed with caramel.
- Have a traditional-looking cake with a choice of different fillings. The top layer should be made of sponge so that the lightest layer is on the top.
- Go for a designer dessert – cake designers can make wonderful novelty cakes, which are particularly good for themed weddings.
- Treat your tastebuds with the sheer indulgence of a chocolate fountain.
- If you're getting married on the beach, hire an ice cream van and treat your guests to whatever ice lolly they fancy.
- Instead of one large cake, why not have lots of little cup cakes iced in white with flowers on top, or in blue for the groom and pink for the bride.
- Tuck into banoffee pie and cream.
- Sponge cakes are always popular. Try a chocolate *sachertorte* served with ice cream.
- Take the biscuit and offer your guests a selection of delicious cookies.

Food and drink checklist

- Will you be having finger food, a buffet or a sit-down meal?
- Does the caterer offer any packages? What is included?
- Is the caterer flexible with menu choices? Can you make suggestions? Will they cater for people with special dietary needs? Will they be able to cater for children?
- How soon can you have a menu tasting?
- What kind of kitchen facilities will be required?
- Are they able to work creatively within your budget?
- Is the serving staff included in the price? What is the ratio of staff to guests? What will the staff wear?
- Have they catered a wedding at your venue before?
- If catering at the bride's home, what kitchen facilities are required and will they take care of all the clearing up?
- How many other bookings do they have for the same day?
- Do they provide all necessary china, glassware and utensils?
- If rental equipment is necessary, who is responsible for its delivery, cleaning and return?
- Will your contact be at the reception to oversee the event?
- When is the final guest count due? Can they accommodate unexpected guests? What is the additional charge?
- What brands of beverages will be served?
- Can you supply your own alcohol? Is there a corkage fee?
- Determine which drinks you would like served when.
- Will the caterer supply extra bar stock like ice, lemons, etc?
- Do they have the correct glassware for the beverages you will be serving?
- Discuss table layout, seating arrangements and the position of the cake table.

- Can they provide staff to look after the cloakroom, place name cards for seating and distribute party favours?
- Is a service charge included or are gratuities optional? Is there a charge for any breakages?
- How far in advance are bookings required?
- How much is the deposit and when is it due?
- How soon after the event is the balance due?
- Is VAT included in the final price?
- What is the policy on cancellation/postponement?
- Confirm dates, times and details with a written contract. Include a breakdown of charges for food, drinks, corkage, staff, delivery, travel expenses, equipment hire and service charges.
- Get insurance.

For the wedding cake
- What type of cake would you like?
- How would you like your cake presented?
- How will it be eaten? Served or taken home?
- Consider the decorations. Will you need fresh flowers or sugar paste? A cake topper? Ribbon?
- How and when will the cake be delivered? Is there a delivery charge?
- Are there appropriate refrigeration facilities on site?
- Are any of your guests allergic to nuts?
- How far in advance should you order the cake?
- How much is the deposit and when is it due?
- How soon after the event is the balance due?
- Is VAT included in the final price?
- What is the policy on cancellation/postponement?
- Confirm dates, times and details with a written contract.
- Get insurance.

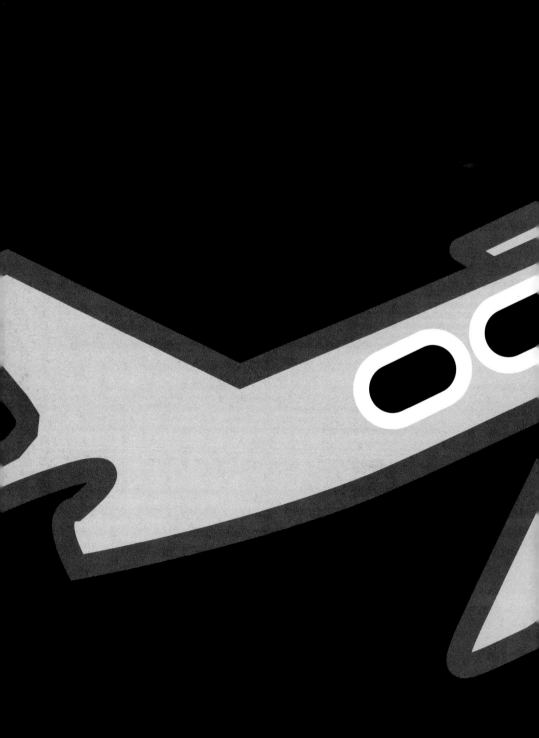

After the
wedding

After the wedding

With all the wedding preparations in full swing, chances are the last thing you want to take on is more planning and organization. When you're planning your wedding it can be difficult to think past the big day, but there is the honeymoon to be organized and other loose ends to be sorted after the main event.

Your honeymoon is going to be one of the most important holidays of your life – you're newlyweds, you want to revel in each other's company and you need to recover from the stresses and strains of planning your wedding. For a honeymoon to remember – for the best reasons – it's worth taking a little time to get it right.

But where do you start? Who should do the organizing, and, more importantly, where should you go? Do you want to lounge on a beach, or would you rather be active? Are you after an island paradise, or do you want to take off on a month-long adventure? This chapter will give you plenty of ideas and inspiration on where to go for your perfect honeymoon.

You'll also need to make sure in advance that all the loose ends will be tied up after your reception, such as returning hire outfits and making sure that presents are put away safely. If you're going on honeymoon straight away, the best thing to do is delegate this to a trusty helper, such as your best man or your parents.

The legal formalities of becoming man and wife – such as changing your name or making a new will – are something else you'll need to consider after the big day.

Planning the honeymoon

Many brides get their husbands to plan and book the honeymoon, for the simple reason that they are usually doing everything else! Traditionally, the groom should foot the bill as well – although most couples now simply share costs. If the groom plans a surprise trip, make sure he gives you an idea of what to expect so that you'll know what to pack and can plan to have all the necessary documentation and vaccinations and medications.

For many couples, planning the trip of a lifetime is one of the most exciting parts of the pre-wedding experience and something they can do without family interference. So even if the groom takes on the research, make it a joint venture and enjoy it.

It takes two

What do you **both** want to do? Make sure that neither of you is simply agreeing to two weeks on a beach to keep the other happy. Remember, too, that you don't have to follow other people's preconceptions about honeymoons. 'Whatever makes you happy' is truly the key.

When planning your honeymoon think about money. In many ways, it's far better to choose a honeymoon that you can easily afford and have enough spending money once you're actually there rather than having to count your pennies all the time.

Honeymoon options

As soon as you have set your wedding date, turn your attention to the honeymoon. You should aim to book it as soon as possible, especially if you're getting married during a peak holiday season, such as July/August or Christmas/New Year.

If you're about to splash out on a 'once-in-a-lifetime' trip, you might even want to set the honeymoon date first. But bear in mind that, although the majority of British weddings take place in June, July and August, this may not be the best time to travel to your chosen destination.

Traditionally, the blushing bride and groom take leave of their guests in the early evening and head off on honeymoon immediately, but most modern couples like to enjoy the whole reception and spend their first married night together in a nearby hotel.

Things to consider

- If you want a quiet, relaxing time together and the stress of long-haul flights isn't your scene, then a remote cottage in Britain may serve you far better than an expensive, all-inclusive, Far Eastern beach holiday.
- For something glamorous and gorgeous, but within your budget, saving on travel in favour of a top-class location may be the best bet. For example, take the train to France and stay in a succession of luxurious châteaux and hotels.

- If a taste of adventure is your scene – whether an African safari, white-water rafting, diving or trekking – make sure you book through a reputable company and that any dangerous activities are properly supervised.
- Perhaps you can think of nothing more romantic than being in St Mark's Square, Venice, or seeing the pyramids. Make sure you do your research and that you know what you can visit and when.
- Walking hand-in-hand through the surf on a white sandy beach is surely the definitive honeymoon scene. Just be sure – especially if you are active types – that you really do both want to be lazing around for the duration of your stay. However, it's possible with many beach holidays to build in some separate activities, and there's no reason why one of you can't scuba dive while the other sunbathes.

- An activity element – perhaps walking, skiing or cycling – can be perfect if you both love the activity involved. After all the stress of the wedding – and all that food and drink – some decent exercise can be invigorating and restorative.
- Although honeymoons are supposed to be romantic, even the most intense lovebirds need some variety! The most popular honeymoon choice nowadays is a 'two-centre' break, combining a week of beach-based relaxation with a more active or city-based week.
- Think carefully before inviting family and friends along on your honeymoon – this is a very special time in your married life and you won't get it again.

Budget or bust

Don't underestimate how exhausted you'll be once the wedding is over. You'll need a good break and it's worth paying a little more to stay somewhere decent. For this reason, last-minute bargain breaks are not really a good idea, unless you really don't mind when and where the honeymoon takes place! Planning well in advance may cost a bit more, but it means you'll get what you really want, when you want it.

Don't add extra stress to the trip by leaving too many elements to chance. Delays are more likely on chartered flights, so you're better off spending your money on scheduled flights instead. You don't want to spend your first night as husband and wife in a departure lounge! Book at least the first week's accommodation up front, plan the itinerary and book your car hire or internal flights. You can even plan and book activities, such as city tours or scuba diving, in advance. Search online for the local tourist board and get some ideas of what you can do while you're away.

Travel insurance is important for peace of mind. Should one of you fall ill, or a theft occur, you'll be covered. Make sure your policy covers the value of wedding and engagement rings.

If you're marrying abroad as well, take out a special wedding policy, which will cover your wedding outfits and gifts.

Build lots of spending money into your budget, so you can indulge in a little luxury. There's not much difference between a four- and five-star hotel – spend the money you save on having fun.

Honeymoon checklist

Three months before the wedding

- By this time you should have booked any flights/package holidays and arranged travel insurance.
- Draw up a basic itinerary and book at least the first few days' accommodation.
- Make sure your passports are valid. If you are changing your name, contact the passport office for the necessary forms.
- Obtain visas, if required.
  - Have all the necessary vaccinations and check whether you need to take malaria tablets.

One month before the wedding

- Finalize your itinerary, pre-book activities, if desired, and confirm hotels in writing.
- Arrange transport from your first-night hotel to the airport and from the airport to home on your return, if applicable.
- Order your foreign currency and travellers' cheques.
- Collect all the necessary paperwork and file it together in a safe place.
- Plan your packing.
- Arrange for someone to collect your wedding clothes from the first-night hotel and store them, or return them to the hire shops.

One week before the wedding

- Collect your currency and travellers' cheques.

One day before the wedding

- Pack and have your luggage taken to the first-night hotel or other convenient point for collection.

Loose ends

Sending thanks

Letters of thanks should be prompt, personal and thoughtful. They may be written by either the bride or groom, or both, usually whoever is closer to the person giving the present. If you have been given cash gifts, it's polite to indicate to the giver how you plan to use the money, or, if you have vouchers, what you have bought or intend to buy with them.

Give that back!

If you call off the wedding, all the presents that you have already received should be offered back to the giver with thanks. No detailed explanations are really necessary.

Changing your name

When a woman marries, she has to decide whether she should change her maiden name and, if so, to what?

There is no legal requirement for a woman to change her surname when she gets married. Upon marriage, there are two automatic legal options available to the woman: she can either continue to use her maiden name or she can take her husband's surname. If she takes her husband's surname, the marriage certificate provides the necessary documentary evidence that she has changed her name.

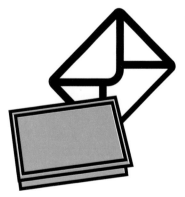

It is becoming increasingly popular for couples to take each other's surname. For example, if Michael Smith marries Susan Brown, they will be known as Michael and Susan Smith-Brown (or Brown-Smith) and will be formally addressed as Mr and Mrs Michael Smith-Brown.

If you decide upon this option and you both wish to have all your records and documents changed, you should both arrange to have your names changed by deed poll after your marriage.

If you choose to use a different name after your marriage, you must advise your bank, employer and other official bodies, such as the Passport Office. It is possible to change the name in your passport before your wedding but your new passport will not be valid until after you are married.

Making a will

Considering making a will at a time of such happiness may seem to be somewhat morbid, but the making of a will is an act of love and consideration undertaken by those who wish to spare their next of kin further pain.

There are two essential prerequisites for a person to make a will: you must be at least 18 years old and be of 'sound mind'. Any existing will is automatically revoked upon marriage, a point that has particular relevance to those remarrying. Therefore, any existing obligations made before the marriage will need to be readdressed to ensure that your wishes are carried out.

Making a will is, for most people, a quick, simple process done through a solicitor or professional will writer and costs are usually quite reasonable. Once completed, you can either lodge it with your solicitor or keep it in a safe place at home or at your bank. You will need to refer to your will only if your circumstances change, such as on the birth of a child or the receipt of a large windfall.

You can purchase do-it-yourself wills from larger stationers. These are legally binding, although probably only suited to those whose estate is very straightforward.

Wedding calendar

At least six months before the wedding

- Decide whether you want a religious or civil ceremony.
- Choose your church or civil venue.
- Decide on an ideal wedding date and time.
- Book service with vicar/priest/registrar. Check fees.
- Arrange a special licence, if necessary.
- Choose reception venue.
- Buy engagement ring – if you haven't done so already!
- Agree budget with father of the bride and decide who is going to pay for what.
- Agree approximate number of guests for ceremony.
- Agree approximate number of guests for reception.
- Agree style and theme of ceremony.
- Agree style and theme of reception.
- Choose your chief bridesmaid, bridesmaids, flower girl and page-boy.

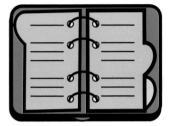

- Groom to choose his best man and ushers.
- Choose witnesses.
- Book reception venue.
- Arrange marquee, if required.
- Make catering arrangements for reception and decide on a menu.
- Book reception entertainment.
- Plan wedding outfits for the bride, bridesmaids, flower girl and page-boy.
- Book dressmaker and shoemaker.
- Order flowers, bouquets, corsages and buttonholes.
- Book photographer and videomaker.

- Draft guest list for ceremony, reception and evening celebrations.
- Book transport for wedding day and going away.
- Insure against disasters, including theft of wedding gifts.
- Book honeymoon and arrange travel insurance.
- Consider a pre-nuptial agreement.

Three months before

- Discuss church/civil ceremony and order of service with the vicar/priest/registrar.
- Discuss music options with the officiant and organist, if applicable.
- Book musicians and singers for ceremony.
- Select items and retailer(s) for gift list.
- Finalize gift list.
- Finalize guest list.
- Prepare map/accommodation details to send out with invitations.
- Order wedding stationery (invitations, order of service sheets, response cards, menus, napkins and place cards).
- Send out invitations with relevant enclosures.
- Create your wedding web pages, including details of the ceremony, reception, guest list, travel and accommodation.
- Buy dresses and outfits, if they're not being made.
- Bride's father and groom to decide on clothes for the men in the wedding party.
- Male members of wedding party to attend clothes fitting.
- Establish dates for publishing banns in both bride's and groom's parish, or notify appropriate register office of intended marriage.
- Buy wedding rings and arrange insurance cover.

- Book reception staff such as toastmaster, if required.
- Order/make wedding cake.
- Plan health and beauty regime, and book appointments.
- Confirm passports are up to date.
- Obtain visas, if required.
- Organize inoculations if marrying or honeymooning abroad. Check if you need to take malaria tablets.
- Arrange to have your passport changed to your married name, if desired.
- Book accommodation for wedding night.

One month before

- Send out details of gift list on request.
- Send thank-you letters for gifts as they arrive.
- Buy shoes, lingerie and accessories.
- Groom, father of the bride and best man to start preparing their speeches.
- If self-catering your wedding, make detailed shopping, cooking and freezing plans.
- Order reception decorations, such as balloons and disposable cameras.
- Collect banns certificate, if marrying in local parish church.
- Check bookings: church/civil venue, florist, photographer, videomaker, transport, hotel, entertainment, cake.
- Arrange a time for wedding rehearsal.
- Buy gifts for the wedding party.
- Arrange for an announcement of your wedding to appear in the local/national press.
- Chase outstanding invitation replies for final numbers.
- Chief bridesmaid to arrange final fitting of bridesmaids' and flower girl's dresses and page-boy's outfits.

- Agree with attendants where they will dress on your wedding day.
- Have practice session with your hairdresser and make appointment for the wedding morning.
- Practise wedding day make-up.
- Chief bridesmaid to arrange hen party.
- Best man to organize stag party, with the help of the ushers, if necessary.
- Arrange safe storage for gifts brought to the reception and for someone to look after them while you're away on honeymoon.
- Check honeymoon arrangements.
- Buy going-away outfits, and clothes and luggage for the honeymoon.
- Arrange for wedding clothes to be collected from first-night hotel and stored/returned to hire shops.
- Order appropriate currency and/or travellers' cheques for the honeymoon.
- Organize honeymoon transport.
- Make arrangements for pets with neighbours or kennels/cattery.

Two weeks before

- Have hair cut/final practice with hairdresser.
- Have final fitting of wedding dress.
- Hen party.
- Stag party.
- Prepare seating plan.
- Meet photographer and videomaker to finalize arrangements.
- Decide first dance and music and inform DJ/band.

- Decide whether to have a receiving line and advise reception venue.
- Inform reception venue and caterers of the final number of guests.
- Advise florist of the final number of buttonholes and corsages.
- Check bride's father, best man and groom have written their speeches.

One week before

- Make a detailed timetable for your wedding day.
- Hold rehearsal with bride, groom, bride's father, best man, bridesmaids, flower girl, page-boy and ushers.
- Wrap gifts for the wedding party and decide when to give them.
- Check arrangements for flowers, cake, entertainment, photographer and transport.
- Decorate wedding cake or arrange to see it at the bakers.
- Advise chief usher of seating plan.
- Father of the bride to check that wedding clothes order is correct and organize collection.
- Do final check on all clothing: try on outfits and wear in wedding shoes.
- Give final confirmation of numbers and any special dietary requirements to reception venue/caterers.
- Do final check on honeymoon plans and any last-minute emergency shopping.
- If you plan to use your car for the wedding and/or honeymoon, check that it's clean and working well.
- Collect foreign currency and travellers' cheques.

One day before

- Make sure best man has a spare set of keys for relevant cars and spare cash.
- Make sure groom has all the messages that need to be read out at the reception.
- Collect any hired clothing and/or accessories.

- Organize delivery of going-away outfit to reception venue/first-night hotel.
- Pack for honeymoon – include clothes, tickets and passports. Have luggage taken to first-night hotel or other convenient location, ready to be picked up the next day.
- Groom to give wedding rings to best man.
- Groom to give fee for the vicar/registrar/organist to best man.
- If you are organizing the reception catering yourself, do any last-minute defrosting and shopping.
- Deliver cake to the venue and arrange to have it assembled.
- Make sure that the going-away car will be in the right place at the right time.
- Lay out your wedding dress, accessories and jewellery.
- Relax and have an early night.

Take advantage of the Confetti interactive wedding calendar at: www.confetti.co.uk

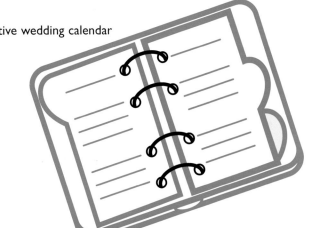

Budget planner

This budget planner will help you to manage the cost of your wedding and avoid any nasty surprises! It also tells you who, traditionally, pays for what, although these days there is greater flexibility over financial responsibility. For an interactive budget planner, check out: www.confetti.co.uk

	Who pays	Your estimate £	Actual cost £
Wedding			
announcements	bride's family		
stationery and postage	bride's family		
church/registrar's fee	groom		
ceremony/music	bride's family		
transport to ceremony and reception (except for groom and best man)	bride's family		
transport to ceremony for groom and best man	groom/groom's family		
flowers for ceremony and reception	bride's family		
bouquets and buttonholes	groom		
gifts for wedding party	bride/groom		
photographer	bride's family		
videomaker	bride's family		
			Total:
Rings			
engagement ring	groom		
bride's wedding ring	groom		
groom's wedding ring	bride		
			Total:

	Who pays	Your estimate £	Actual cost £
Fashion and beauty			
wedding dress/outfit	bride's family		
veil/headdress/hat	bride's family		
bride's shoes and accessories	bride's family		
skincare/hairdressing/make-up	bride		
bride's going-away outfit	bride's family		
groom's suit/accessories	groom's family		
bridesmaids' dresses and accessories	bride's family		
flower girl's and page-boy's outfits	bride's family		
			Total:
Reception			
hire of venue/marquee/equipment	bride's family		
wedding cake	bride's family		
entertainment	bride's family		
catering, food and drink	bride's family		
			Total:
Honeymoon			
first-night accommodation	groom		
travel and accommodation	groom		
spending money	bride / groom		

GRAND TOTAL:

Index

About confetti.co.uk

Confetti.co.uk, founded in 1999, is the leading destination for brides- and grooms-to-be. Every month over 700,00 people visit www.confetti.co.uk to help them plan their weddings and special occasions. Here is a quick guide to our website

Weddings The wedding channel is packed full of advice and ideas to make your day more special and your planning less stressful. Our personalized planning tools will ensure you won't forget a thing.

Celebrations Checklists, advice and ideas for every party and celebration.

Fashion and beauty View hundreds of wedding, bridesmaid and party dresses and accessories. Get expert advice on how to look and feel good.

Travel Search for the most idyllic destinations for your honeymoon, wedding abroad or romantic breaks. Get fun ideas for hen and stag weekends.

Suppliers Thousands of suppliers to choose from including venues, gift lists companies, cake makers, florists and bridal retailers.

Café Talk to other brides and grooms and get ideas from our real life weddings section. Ask Aunt Betti, our agony aunt, for advice.

Shop All your wedding and party essentials in one place. The ranges include planning essentials, books and CDs, personalised stationery for weddings and celebrations, create your own trims, ribbons and papers, table decorations, party products including hen and stag, memories and gifts. If you'd like to do your shopping in person or view all the ranges before buying online, please visit the confetti stores.

Online

- Shop online 24 hours a day 7 days a week, use quick searches by department, product code or keyword, use the online order tracking facility and view brand new products as soon as they come out.
- Shop by phone on 0870 840 6060 Monday to Friday between 9 am and 5 pm.
- Shop by post by sending a completed order form to Confetti, Freepost NEA9292, Carr Lane, Low Moor, Bradford, BD12 0BR or fax on 01274 805 741.

By phone/freepost

Request your free copy of our catalogue online at www.confetti.co.uk or call 0870 840 6060

In store

London – 80 Tottenham Court Road, London, W1T 4TE

Leeds – The Light, The Headrow, Leeds, LS1 8TL

Birmingham – 43 Temple Street, Birmingham B2 5DP

Glasgow – 15–17 Queen Street, Glasgow, G1 3ED

Reading – 159 Friar Street, Reading, RG1 1HE

Executive Editor **Katy Denny**
Managing Editor **Clare Churly**
Executive Art Editor **Penny Stock**
Design **Cobalt id**
Production Manager **Ian Paton**